THE BIMBO ANTHOLOGY

Editors

Madison Whatley
Yael Valencia Aldana

Purple Ink Press

Hollywood,
Florida

Purple Ink Press
5924 Sheridan Street, No. 2128
Hollywood, Florida, 33021
www.purpleinkpress.com

The Bimbo Anthology / edited
by Madison Whatley and Yael Valencia Aldana,
 -- 1st ed.
ISBN 979-8-9892793-3-3

Cover image by Pawel Szymanski
Cover design and interior design by Yael Valencia Aldana

To all the Bimbos, Himbos, and Thembos making their mark.

ME by Carolyn Schlam

Table of Contents

Introduction

What is a Bimbo anyway? It's a word people throw at you to make you feel stupid. A word people throw at you when they find you attractive but stupid. Merriam-Webster dictionary defines Bimbo as "informal + disparaging: woman; especially an attractive but vacuous woman. 2. dated slang, usually disparaging." Dictionary.com defines a Bimbo as "a foolish, stupid, or inept person. a man or fellow, often a disreputable or contemptible one." It's one of those words people say to make you feel like crap. A friend told me a family friend called her a Bimbo when she was a child. Well, we are reclaiming Bimbo, taking it back and making it ours. A Bimbo is what we make it. We are Bimbos because we are unique. We define our lives. We might be Bimbos, Himbos, or Thembos. Yeah, we like sex, and sometimes we don't. We are us! Yeah, we are messy and figuring it out, but we are powerful, and mad, and happy and pissed off, soft, and creative.

When we posted the call for this anthology, people showed up, a lot of people. We were surprised, especially because we hadn't defined our vision of the new Bimbo. We were floored by the incredible submissions we received. And we knew we hit a sweet spot when the poet Chen Chen posted that he was a Himbo.

We are so excited to share this collection.
Bimbos-Himbo-Thembos reporting for duty!

–Yael

Beach by Marvin Meyer

Femina by Carolyn Schlam

tess

by Eleni Gemitzis

---

this almost-shy *thump*. god, to break your neck on the fourth-floor window! a sparrow. i get up from my desk, and the whirring of the fan finally gives way to something else. lethargic motor buzzing and glimmering heat now ooze through the window. no wonder: all feverish birds. how to live in that slowness? yet: no death on the windowsill, none ten metres below on the sidewalk. the tram sluggishly grinds ahead, and so does august,

in its sickening ways. a message from tess; *we can grab food and drinks at the max-eyth lake and sit in the deckchairs there if you like* and yes, i'd like that, although one cannot possibly know whether she looks forward to it really or performs only

to label us as friends. nobody is paying close enough attention anyway. forty minutes to the other side of town and we hug at the tram stop, collarbones and shoulders, and we talk about the weather and the greylag geese who sleep with open eyes. the way to the shore is long,

the menu overwhelmingly packed. she likes my outfit; i struggle with *thank you*, then manage. we share fries, and both order lillet, although i know she prefers beer. she shows me pictures of the flat she and mo will be moving into. i last saw him at tess's birthday party. drunk conversations of different friend groups that i wasn't a part of, well-intentioned drinks tess kept pouring me; i danced.

you can't tell mo not to shit her friends accused her. *i can* she insisted, *and i already am.* a heated debate on projection broke loose. tess ended up reviewing laxatives. she didn't want to look fat next to him, to be as heavy on him as he was on her, and none of it made sense to anyone. i remembered

how she had kissed my belly, grabbed my thigh, fat and everywhere. during the discussion, mo was leaning onto some table in the distance. he probably couldn't hear what the fuss was about but tess,

tess was a crystal that night, a loupe exposing it all. *what I've been wondering* i reveal, *is whether it was really you who wanted to do what we did back then, or a projection.* she laughs, *what* did *we do?* she's teasing, i think, then suddenly become aware of our surroundings. laugh half-heartedly, don't admit i really need that answer. smiles within kisses, intertwined fantasies, her tongue on my armpit. some curiosity and confirmed suspicions later – i don't know how else to put it – we would meet for coffee occasionally and always send out birthday invitations. finally:

i wanted it, of course. all deckchairs but ours have emptied. we discover neither of us know older couples who kiss each other. properly, that is. suddenly, uncontrollable disgust towards the algae in the lake. how haven't i noticed before? goosebumps, the setting sun. are we actively avoiding eye contact? *how can anyone swim in here* i say. her gaze hits me with strange urgency. *it's prohibited, the algae. oh* i answer, *i see.*

my tram squeaks into place as we reach the station, *see you soon*, chest to chest. there are no conclusions on the drive home. as i walk from the final stop through the darkness, i see my fourth-floor window left wide open from afar. still no sign of the sparrow as i approach the front door.

V.S.

by Jennifer Maritza McCauley

Candy-venomed,
saccharine, tangled
licorice, gallows-deep.

I ran off yesterday,
broke the ribbon-line,
told you: follow the
hemline of my fresh
dress, it's bright
as shadow.

I got licked in the last fight,
damn right.

Still, I came back scream-smiling.
Look: I found out you were tall
as bullet.

So I bit the length of this journey off,
got soft as preening fire, entiendes?

I'm sweet-skinned and horrible.

You can call me any other name
but I call myself

viper/sweet.

She COULD therefore She Did by Kathy Bruce

Kinky

by Denise Duhamel

They decide to exchange heads.
Barbie squeezes the small opening under her chin
over Ken's bulging neck socket. His wide jaw line jostles
atop his girlfriend's body, loosely,
like one of those novelty dogs
destined to gaze from the back windows of cars.
The two dolls chase each other around the orange Country Camper
unsure what they'll do when they're within touching distance.
Ken wants to feel Barbie's toes between his lips,
take off one of her legs and force his whole arm inside her.
With only the vaguest suggestion of genitals,
all the alluring qualities they possess as fashion dolls,
up until now, have done neither of them much good.
But suddenly Barbie is excited looking at her own body
under the weight of Ken's face. He is part circus freak,
part thwarted hermaphrodite. And she is imagining
she is somebody else—maybe somebody middle class and ordinary,
maybe another teenage model being caught in a scandal.

The night had begun with Barbie getting angry
at finding Ken's blow up doll, folded and stuffed
under the couch. He was defensive and ashamed, especially about
not having the breath to inflate her. But after a round
of pretend-tears, Barbie and Ken vowed to try
to make their relationship work. With their good memories
as sustaining as good food, they listened to late-night radio
talk shows, one featuring Doctor Ruth. When all else fails,
just hold each other, the small sex therapist crooned.
Barbie and Ken, on cue, groped in the dark,
their interchangeable skin glowing, the color of Band-Aids.
Then, they let themselves go— Soon Barbie was begging Ken

to try on her spandex miniskirt. She showed him how
to pivot as though he was on a runway. Ken begged
to tie Barbie onto his yellow surfboard and spin her
on the kitchen table until she grew dizzy. Anything,
anything, they both said to the other's requests,
their mirrored desires bubbling from the most unlikely places.

Originally published in Denise's book *Kinky* (1997) by Orchises Press.

Untitled by Jessica Felicio

Untitled by Marvin Meyer

Writing an Erotic Romance Novel

by Melissa Ford Lucken (Isabelle Drake)

As you know, the only thing that matters about an erotic romance novel is the book's cover image. For your erotic romance, the image should be a man's chest, his bare chest, maybe including his belt, undone, and the lowered waistband of his jeans. Do not include much of what is below said belt; if you do, Walmart will not carry your book. No. That is not a joke. Also, do not include anything above his neck. It doesn't matter who he is. Walmart doesn't care, either. We all want him to represent The Any-man. Not any man, exactly. An idealized representation of what any man could look like. If he didn't have a job or family, and worked out every day, all day, for at least seven years. You may have thought about having a woman on the book cover. Maybe you thought a story about a woman should have a woman on the cover.

Do not include a woman. Her body will be too sensual, too sexual, and Walmart will not carry your book. No. That is not a joke. Then again, never mind all that. You don't need to worry about the cover image, as you will not select it. The cover art department will pick it.

What's that? Are you concerned about the cover image representing what is actually in your novel? You are alone in that worry. The cover art department is hooked up with the marketing department and well, we all know what marketing cares about. Money. Maybe you care about money, too. Why else would you be writing an erotic romance? Certainly not because you want to write something readers will want to read. Not because you actually care about love, romance, happiness. It's because you read all of, part of, or heard about, *Fifty Shades of Grey*, and know that if *she* can get rich and famous quickly and easily, you can, too.

In the text, you will want to use a lot of dirty words. All the dirty words you can think of. The words don't need to be listed here because you already know them. The list contains all the 'bad' words you say when you're angry. It includes the 'naughty' words used in the telling of off-color jokes. It also includes the others. The ones you know but never say aloud. Maybe you don't even think about them. But you *know* them and all the others. That's all there is to it—just the words. Don't bother agonizing about plot structure, scene structure, character interiority, creating a vivid setting, or even doing any research to ensure your story has a reality to it. Erotic romance novels don't need reality.

Eroticism isn't a real thing. It isn't something anyone ever aspires to in real life. No one even cares about it. No one cares about romance, either, not one bit. That's why the romance novel genre is consistently among the top-selling in the book market. Top selling means top money, and so, you see, we are back to being all about the cash. And the fame. The glorious, glorious fame of being an author of erotic romance. Before that fame, there is a tiny bit of work to be done. Once you have the list of dirty words, you are ready to begin.

While you are writing the pages, expect to have pink-scented candles lit and glowing gently, chilled bottles of champagne standing by, ready for sipping, and access to endless inspirations, memories, from your own sensational, madcap experiences to bring the story to life. Yes, of course, those inspirations come from *your own* real-life adventures: menage sex, group sex, trips to BDSM clubs, strip clubs, and swingers' clubs. Also, extensive experience with all forms of sex toys. Also, sex in cars, sex in barns, sex on boardroom tables. Sex while standing. Sex while sitting. Sex while dancing. Sex on street corners. Sex in spaceships. Sex on pirate ships. Sex on row boats. Sex on millionaires' boats. Sex on Viking boats. Sex beside a castle moat. Sex on horseback. Sex on motorcycles (while traveling at speeds over 50 miles per hour.) And all the rest of your long, extensive list of *experiences*.

While writing, toss in words from the list to make the action more vivid. More descriptive. More accurate. Unlike writers of other genres, and for the sake of argument, we will include literary works as a genre, and you will not need to rely on imagination, craft, or creativity. You will simply write down every sexual act you have ever done and then change the names of those involved. If you never knew the others' names or have forgotten them, this is not a problem. Make some up.

Filling the pages with the words that recreate your own, exhilarating, uninhibited, sex life, then selling said story and guiding it into publication, complete with its distinctive any-man cover, won't be the slightest bit difficult. Writing a romance novel, especially an erotic romance novel, is not anything writers do with intention. No writers dream of telling a story about passionate characters who come together and commit themselves to each other despite all odds. This sort of thing, love, happiness, and connecting with other humans, these are not things anyone cares about or is interested in. So, don't bother with first-rate crafting or meticulous character development. Luckily, evoking emotion is easy—especially the complicated feelings involved with emotional and physical intimacy. Just keep writing words until you have 70,000 of them. No heart-wrenching revising.

No painstaking editing. Getting that 70K down will take...say...two weeks?

Three weeks tops. Once the pages are filled with words, things will continue moving so quickly and easily that you won't even have time to tweet about it. Getting an agent, an afternoon. Maybe, at the absolute most, an entire day. Simply email every agent listed on agentquery.com before 9:00 am EST. You will get dozens of offers for representation by lunchtime. Or by dinner time.

Before slipping into bed, sign with the agent most likely to buy you many pretty martinis when you go to New York to sign your multiple book deal from one of the New York's Big Five Publishers. Getting that deal? That'll take a bit longer. One week. Maybe two—if the editors are all off at the Hamptons and too hung over to check their email.

Once the contract is signed, you will be busy. You won't have to arrange your own book signings or send out your own press releases. You won't have to create your own social media accounts or interact with romance readers. You won't be lugging boxes of books to event halls or sweating in the sun at outdoor book festivals. You won't spend hours at the keyboard writing that second book in the series. You will be busy getting interviewed by book bloggers, podcasters, and Jules Buono, who hosts the Good Morning America book club. The interviewers, except Jules Buono, who will have actually read your book, will ask, "So...where do you get your, wink wink, *inspiration*?" This question won't be offensive at all. The interviewers won't be smirking as they ask it. They won't be staring at you...oddly, and fortunately, you will have the answer—the right answer. The wrong answer would be, "I craft characters who...." (anything after that phrase). Or, "I start by doing research on... (again, anything after that phrase is wrong). What is the right, desired response is what is true. You simply write down all of your own sexual experiences—then change the names. Maybe the setting, too. Also, perhaps the time period. Also, what you did. You change that. You make it something someone else did. Or something no one ever did. As long as the interviewer gets the opportunity to make sex jokes and minimize your work because it contains sex and has a happy ending, everything will be fine unless you expect to be respected as an author. Then, well, you will be disappointed.

Fortunately, that course to disappointment will only be limited to strangers. Your family and close friends will totally and completely respect and admire your perseverance and dedication. After all, they have been cheering you on, supporting you, encouraging and understanding you each and every time you chose to "work on that romance book thing" instead of helping them clean out their garage. Now that the "romance book thing" is out and getting read and reviewed (by strangers), they are even more supportive. They are even proud. They are so proud that they are embarrassed and joke about you and your work. That's if they acknowledge it at all. (No, of course, they have not read it. They don't need to. They have seen the any-man chest. They know the secret about your *experiences*.) They show their pride in your accomplishment by offering thoughtful encouragement such as, "I get that it took a couple of weeks to write, but with all those sex scenes in there, it must have been easy." Although you don't realize it, that is a funny thing to say. You know this because they are laughing. You aren't laughing. But wait, there is more.

When you run into them during the holidays, it turns out they wonder about that second book you are already "messing around with" and ask, while looking at you oddly, "Where are you going to get *inspiration* for another one?" You are thinking about the character charts you have created. You are thinking about that research you have begun.

Meanwhile, they are wondering, surely, that one book, the one that is already out and getting read and reviewed by strangers, contains all of your wild, passionate, fulfilling, exquisite sexual experiences? Surely you could not have had more wild, more passionate, more fulfilling, and more exquisite sexual experiences than they have had? That would be sad. That would be unfair. That would make them feel…you don't know what, but you do know that feeling is something they do not want to feel. And this is the most important part so pay attention, it is totally and completely your fault that they are feeling it. Whatever it is. The two of you ponder about this terrible thing you have done. That moment is the exact moment you both think the same thing. *I don't want to talk with you about this topic ever again.* There is a terrible pause, and then one of you thinks about getting back to that third round of binge-watching *Game of Thrones*; the other speculates about the any-man chest image that will appear on the cover of that next book, the one you are already "messing around with."

Yes, of course, it's you who is the one speculating about that new cover. You walk away, hoping the next conversation at this holiday gathering will not be about your *inspirations* or *experiences*.

What you really want is to tell someone that this whole thing of writing the erotic romance novel and being an esteemed author of romance fiction is not what you expected. That someone you finally find to tell isn't a family member or a friend.

It's me.

You don't find out about me until you're lugging your leftover any-man chest-covered books out of a convention hall after a signing. You're a tad tired. You've been smiling, passing out your custom-designed swag, and inscribing your erotic romance novels for three hours. You bump into me, and for no reason in particular, except that we are both esteemed, respected authors of erotic romance, we start chatting. Celebrating. Commiserating. We end up at the bar. We order pretty martinis and invite other weary but esteemed erotic romance authors to join us.

You decide I must know a thing or two about the book business. And about the untamed, exotic, experience-filled life of an erotic romance author. You ask me, did I know it was *going to be like this*? The looks. Investigations into *the experiences*. Family and friends are looking at you...oddly, acting...weird. Is weird is another word for rude, you ask. You aren't sure. It's been a long day. I take a sip of my pretty martini, set the glass down, and then tell you, no, I didn't know.

Another esteemed author of erotic romance, she's drinking a can of Diet coke, tells you that no, she didn't know either. There are nods around the table, followed by boisterous but dark laughter. I see a familiar black cloud of doubt and despair pass over your face.

I wait until the laughter fades, then tell you something you have discovered, maybe without realizing it—writing romance, erotic romance is serious business. The agents know it. They will get your work to the right publisher. The publishers know it. They will get your work onto the physical and virtual shelves. But the people who are most serious about your work are the readers.

They are as serious as a week at the beach. The right book in their hands, they will tell you, make their hard-earned vacation days perfect. Reading your steamy love story will give them the break they need so they can return to their chaotic life refreshed and ready. They are as serious as a mother of two seated beside her own mother's hospital bed. The right book in their hands, they will tell you, distract them from the despair so they can last through another night of worry. The readers are as serious about appreciating your hard work of writing as they are about their hard work of living.

I take the final sip of my pretty martini and say, if you are after that money, chasing that glorious fame, or simply want to write a good book that people want to read, think about the readers. They will not look at you oddly. They will not ask speculative questions about your *experiences*. All they want to know is the release date of your next any-man chest image-covered book.

Writing an Erotic Romance Novel: Author's Note

Isabelle Drake was born in the spring of 2005. After five years of publishing mainstream romances with small presses, I'd received a contract for my first erotic romance, *Everglades Wildfire*. I used a pseudonym not because I was embarrassed about penning an erotic romance but because I wanted to enjoy the creative process of writing. I'd been trying to sell my manuscripts to The Big Publishers for years and had come heart-breakingly close on several occasions; publishing the steamy stuff in silence reconnected me with my love of writing and telling stories.

50 Shades of Grey wouldn't shake up the book world for six years, but romance readers were already making their desire for steamy reads known. Five years before I came on the scene, a publisher that would at its high point be recognized as the world's largest publisher of erotic romance released its first books—sold on floppy discs. Its founder, Jaid Black, was told by The Big Publishers that no women would be interested in reading anything that smutty, so she started her own publishing company, Ellora's Cave. Many authors started with EC: Sylvia Day and Isabelle Drake, for example.

Readers and reviewers ravished the new steamy reads. Wanting in on the quick-growing market, bookstores began to grant the erotic romances shelf space, but it's likely that Ereaders such as the Kindle made sales skyrocket. A person who wanted a sex-forward story could buy it within minutes and in the privacy of their own home. By the time everyone on the planet was fussing over *50 Shades of Grey*, we authors of erotic romance, and our fans were already years into the bookish heatwave.

Amidst that, along comes another wave: reconnecting via the godfather of social media, Facebook. And suddenly, people who knew me, Melissa Ford Lucken, were finding out I was also Isabelle Drake— esteemed and successful author of fiction (some erotic romance, some not) and that I'd been publishing for years. Surrounded by other hard-working authors and dedicated, happy readers, I didn't find what I was doing scandalous, insignificant, easy, or worthy of ridicule. What did they, these freshly reacquainted folks of my past, think? Well, the essay answers that.

–Melissa Ford Lucken

Untitled by Cottonbro Studio

Voices

by Jennifer Maritza McCauley

I am the voice hollering on the side corner
I am the voice whispering under the short jamb
I am the voice speaking slants to new companions
I am the voice talking mid-level at the podium

My voice drifts like sludge-slow river
My voice has a slicing edge
My voice is soft as little baby's fabric
My voice is raging like ripping flame

I claim all of my voices
They breathe and wriggle and press against me
Even if you don't understand
Why this smiling Black girl
Spits these heaving sentences

These voices tell me to fire on.

Untitled by Cottonbro Studio

Henry Rollins Was My First Girlfriend
Henry Rollins Was My First Boyfriend

by Joe Hilliard

Henry Rollins was always in bed with us. Black Flag playing all the time. The boombox I got as a graduation present from my parents next to the dorm room bed. Cassettes splayed all over the floor. Us splayed all over the bed. Tangled in the covers. Tangled in each other. Haydee's breasts in my mouth. Her hand on my throbbing cock. Our lips locked. Henry in our ears. Henry splayed all over the bed. Henry tangled in the covers in our minds in my mind. Haydee's breasts in his mouth. His hand on my throbbing cock. My mouth on his on hers on his. On his throbbing cock. It's 1990, who knows what's going on? I know I didn't.

It's cliché to say every couple has a song. I think it's a teenage infatuation. You get all caught up and everything is bright and vibrant. Dangerous and cool. One moment lasting a few seconds, lasting forever. Haydee was the only relationship that had a song. Later ones would have soundtracks, mixtapes, but that first big romance, it had a song. One song. Sure, Black Flag was playing. "Damaged" was the album. Side 2, the Henry side. "Damaged I" was the song. You're here with me now, I would growl. I would whisper it in her ear. As I tossed her back onto the pillows. Buy your ticket, she purred, and wait for your turn, she would reply. It was always our turn. Always rushing from class to strip down to nothing in her dorm room, revel in our nakedness. Give me your everything. I'll bite!. Repeated to each other. As we bit each other. Nipples. Thighs. Toes. Pounding Greg Ginn guitars. Snarling Henry. Gasping Haydee. Moaning me. Henry staring straight into us.

We had a scratchy print bootleg video of Richard Kern's "The Right Side of

My Brain" with Rollins and Lydia Lunch. Straight from Hong Kong with a bunch of early Tsui Hark films. It had Chinese subs across the bottom. Better than a Japanese print, which may have had clearer picture quality, but would have still been fuzzed for pubic nudity. I had a print of Jodorowsky's "El Topo" that was censored just so. Topless was AOK, but bottomless, not so much. And we all lived bottomless. We would play the Kern, Black Flag looping. Rewind. Repeat. Sometimes I still dream of that time. Warm spring in Ann Arbor. Sometimes I am Henry. Sometimes I am Lydia. Sometimes I am me. Sometimes I am Haydee. I never told her. About Henry. Not the part of me that wanted Henry. About being her. It was 1990. All I wanted was to please, and be pleased.

We went out for two years, hiding from the cold Ann Arbor winters under the cover of blankets and Black Flag. We bit. We clawed. We smothered our lips over every inch of each other. She blew me. Bit my nipples. Slapped me in the face. Henry wailed. She slid two fingers up my ass. I devoured her juices. Bit her toes. Pinched her nipples. Spanked her ass with a wooden hairbrush she kept on the nightstand between the cassettes and panties and tawdry trade paperback sized porn story magazines Haydee had my purchase at the bookstore downtown. While she waited outside in the snow. I would read them aloud to her, with video flaring and the punk rock flowing. The power of words. The sway of language. The mingling of sight and sound and noise. Rewind. Repeat. Words flowing, guitars riffing, the black and white flickering over us in the twilight.

It took me almost twenty years to finally sleep with a guy. We met online. I wish I could say it was more romantic. But it was built-up lust. It was Craigslist. It wasn't 1990. It was 2010. Everything at your fingertips. He was a punk guy. He didn't look like Henry, more like Wattie from the Exploited. My fingers tight in his thickly-sprayed mohawk as he went down on me for the first time. Trying not to tear a spike out. Trying not to scream out. "I'll bite it off." Finding myself, just finding myself, on the carpet, between his thighs. No one had boomboxes anymore. Now it was a cd of "Damaged" that skipped where it had a dent in it. And I bit my lip as he penetrated me and Henry screamed and I screamed and he screamed and the juices flowed. Down my thigh. Down my chest. Down his chest. And Henry's bare sweaty chest as concert footage played on his laptop, tech so high tech. And yet not. Because of the flesh. The soft supple of the flesh. Lon's lips on mine, that sweaty year we were in and out of each other's lives, in and out of each other's mouths, in and out of each other's ass. Rewind. Repeat. Raining screaming kisses and the deep pound of Henry Rollins. It was 2010. All I wanted was to please, and be pleased.

Henry screams out it's only in his mind. Perhaps, no one cums in. But that's not true. Not for me. Not here. It's not 1990 anymore. It's not 2010 anymore. Sometimes I need a little focus. Sometimes I need a little inspiration. Sometimes I need a little Henry in me. Sometimes metaphorically. Sometimes metaphysically. And yes, sometimes literally. Sexi es todo. All I want is to please. It's simply everything...

Untitled by Anna Shvets

A Song of the Hypermasculine

by Arnaldo Batista

Polo shirts, cargo shorts, crew necks, and muscles.
Shocker fingers, finger blasts, backwards hats, muscles.

Peacocking, sweaty pits, swamp ass, deadlifts.
Gym grunts, sex hunts, baseball bats, muscles.

Hercules, Atlas, Hephaestus, Ares.
Take a load off, grab a Pabst, flex our muscles.

Sauna room, cold pools, quick glance, no homo.
Public showers, loose towels, show our tats and muscles.

That's gay, I don't swing that way, go away, faggot.
Masc4Masc, no Femmes no Fats, unless you got some muscles.

Coming In

by Frances Koziar

"So," my mom said at breakfast toward the end of grade 10, sitting down beside me where I sat twirling a spoon in a half-eaten bowl of cereal. "Jessie and Nakisha came out, huh?"

I grunted. My two best friends had come out in the fall, one as aromantic and the other as a lesbian, and I still couldn't stop thinking about it. For all the memes and motivational speeches and celebrities that said otherwise, I didn't think coming out was a good idea. High school was hard enough without that.

"They seem happy," my mother offered.

"I guess," I muttered, staring at my bowl. I thought of how my eldest sister had learned that the childhood friends she'd lost contact with were both in teacher's college now, like her. *I guess we were more the same than we knew*, she had said, smiling and lifting her hands in a shrug.

The knot was in my gut again, twisting like sickness. My mom left me alone and went to her room, and I felt relief and shame at the same time.

My friends *were* happy. They seemed freer and more confident. Me, on the other hand…I was a mess. One day, I felt envious; the next, lonely; the third, sad; the fourth, scared of what would happen to them, even though nothing did. And in between those, I would wake in the night, feeling anxious about something I hadn't even done, about just the idea of wearing the heels I'd loved as a boy into school, or wearing a dress, or doing anything that might expose me to the hate I'd seen toward queer people on the internet.

I snapped awake to the sound of an Amazon box being plopped down on the kitchen counter.

"What is it?" I asked my mom, suddenly worried that this would be an awkward parent moment and she'd ordered condoms or something.

"Just some clothing I'm going to return if you don't want them. Try them on," she said with a smile. And then she was gone, up to work on the computer in her room, leaving me alone in a silent house.

I reached out tentatively toward the brown packing paper, like there would be a viper below it, and yet I felt hope, too, if that makes sense. The moment I saw the clothing, I dropped it and leapt back. Then, I automatically looked both ways in case someone had seen it.

"Mom!" I breathed, meaning to shout it but saying it more like a curse under my breath instead. I wanted to tell her that I wanted nothing to do with hot pink fishnet stockings, but I was alone in the kitchen. I grabbed my backpack, my phone, and I left for school, walking so fast that my calves burned.

All through the day, that box distracted me, and the last thing I wanted to see was that it had been moved to my room when I got home.

I didn't know if I was trans or gay or just non-gender conforming, I didn't know how I felt or what I wanted, but I *did* know that I didn't want to tell the world about it the way my friends had.

But I looked further into the box. Saw the strapless sports bra, too.

Considered that it would hug my skin. Considered that the stockings could be hidden under pants.

Three bad sleeps and a fight with my mom later, I tried on the clothes. My door was locked, the house empty, and my eyes were on the closed window blinds. I took them off immediately.

A week later, I left the house wearing them under jeans and a thick jacket. It was the scariest thing I'd ever done. I froze on the sidewalk outside my house, about to run back in, but then someone saw me and I had to walk with them.

I could hardly think all morning, terrified that someone would notice. I don't know when the fear became excitement.

When I got home from school, I fingered the fishnet under my jeans, and ran up to the mirror in my room. Staring at myself, and how I looked like an ordinary gender-conforming boy on the outside, I felt tears prick my eyes. It was like coming out but only on the inside. I still didn't understand anything, but I did know that suddenly I couldn't stop grinning, and that the tension in my gut was gone.

Echo Pleas
after Ellie Gomero

by Arnaldo Batista

Biding my time/by the bathroom/of the bar/where I string/men along a wire/
and dangle them/from their scalps/their feet that kick/and kick/and kick/and all I
want/here/is to love them/to wear them like clothes/or a silver chain/I keep at my
neck/my heart that quakes/them every so often/my heart that moves/them/like
water in a creek/the settling/of their bodies/in the riverbed/of my chest/like silt/or
clay/or a man/who settles/because he's unsure/as unsteady/as the ocean/but/won't
you forgive me?

Untitled by Caique Nascimento

Cuz This Bitch Comes with a Warning Label

by Anyély Gómez-Dickerson

**Note: Proceed at Your Own Risk*

Cuz they say I'm like...
Too loud / que chusma ...just cuz I get excited
Too aggressive / que violenta ...just for being assertive
Too rude / que maleducada ...when I speak Spanish or whateva
Too slutty / que mujerzuela ...when I rock my red lipstick
Too vindictive / que venenosa ...when I demand an eye for an eye
Too combative / que agresiva ...when I voice any opinion
Too moody / que hipócrita ...when I change my mind
Too bossy / que caprichosa ...when I ask for what I want
Too arrogant / que vanidosa ...when I'm feeling good about myself
Too jealous / que envidiosa ...if I don't overlook betrayal
Too selfish / que aprovechadora ...when I want my fair share
Too gossipy / que chismosa ...if I share with a friend
Too offensive / que sucia ...when my hips sway in tight jeans

So what am I to do to comfort you? Stop being so excited and assertive?
Only wear what you deem appropriate? Learn to speak only when spoken to?
Only talk in your tongue, never mine? Squash all my opinions, feelings, and wants?
Burn my tight jeans? Toss the lipstick? Turn my back on all my friends?
Live in a prison of your making? A cell only you have the key to.
That's whatchu want. You want to look. You want the lipstick, the jeans, the slut.
But you want it all to yourself... ...and only when you want it.

You wanna own, control, use, and discard—rinse, wash, repeat. But not on my watch!
Cuz this Bitch comes with a warning label or haven't you heard?
I am...loud, aggressive, rude, slutty, vindictive, combative, moody,
bossy, arrogant, jealous, selfish, gossipy, and offensive
so how can you possibly handle all this? *¡Dime!*

The answer is you can't
cuz I won't let you,
cuz I'm all of those things
and much much more.

And aren't you lucky
I come with a warning label.

El Chiste Interno en Río Piedras
(The Inside Joke)

by Jennifer Maritza McCauley

Hey, mamita
speak Spanish out of the wet
part of your
cheek, nena, open
those lips
for the university calle.

Fit your mouth
like a tobacco man ready to
spit, yeah
Get a little bass in that throat
if you want to sound
como una morena actual
They'll call you negra en secreto but for now
you are morena, to be polite.

This is politeness, in color, in your
Mami's homeplace,
amongst
Your own gente, who will always
pick the lightest girls.

Anyway.
Guiño guiño   wink   wink
Guiño guiño   wink   wink

Get ready to dance for some new man-hips
who have never seen a girl who can
mezclar that color and chat weird like you,
They'll say: let's see this negra

whip and shake.

Fit your mouth for the San Juan
streets after they've been stamped
on by los Estados Unidos, your
homeplace, you of the Blackest
privilege.

Yo
cantocantocantocanto
Puñetaaaapuñpun   pun

Here's the inside joke, morena-negra
negra americana.

Speak well, if you wanna survive,
speak that lengua
right.

Untitled by Deji Akinyele

cuz i am

by Anyély Gómez-Dickerson

girly eyelashes & rough intestines

a coffee-soaked soul & cassava hips

northward & south-facing with apple pie

y hot café con leche flavors i watch my palm trees

shiver in the snowfall as pangs of pride urge me

toward the infinite stardust of my 1's and 0's

cuz i am

a brick fortress & a melted puddle

all decked out in denim y Santería beads

with Madonna lace y Cubaton syncopation

tangled up in my Shakespeare & my Neruda

i live as a wanderer & a homebody

i am the whore & the mother

the ancestral ghost & the daughter

i am the nightmare & the cure

the queen wrapped in a rebel with the power

of all the deepest oceans & the thirst

of all the forgotten deserts

i am clean clothes on the clothesline

as quiet blood spills from a secret life of dirty laundry

into my hamper smeared with lust & rage i sing

from my cage breathing Elton John y Celia Cruz
as my lungs inhale/exhale his piano y los timbales
en Espanish or Inglés living between aquí y allá

cuz beneath the landscape of my sugar skin
life remains innocent with a few scrapes & scars
here & there but smooth to my touch & i touch it
cuz beneath the landscape of my sweet sugar skin
flows the elixir that once ruled over all things
& from the source i drink it

& beneath my chipped hot-pink fingernails
a line of dignity remains for i am womb,
pinnacle, deathbed & tomb
Lost. Split & Disconnected.
Broken. Found & Cemented.
i am all things & i celebrate it

Untitled by Samuel Nuñez

Puerto Rican Manic Pixie Dream Girl

by Jennifer Maritza McCauley

I'll fit directly in your pocket, trust'ame. Make me into your ever-beaming muñeca, call me something candy-colored like cocoa-caramel-mocha something-something, slick the way I sweat, marvel at the way I trip and leap and blush. Take stock of my sweaters, shirts something tribal and suggestive of a place you'd know better if you researched about it but you won't. Tell me to talk that Spanish slow, in chunks or slants, steal a word and say it back as if you're spitting it. Make me call you Papi chulo and teach you how to salsa, though I'll do it with a little silly sway. Touch my hair, violet or pink, tell me you like it best when I'm wigged out.

You'll ask me about Derrida too. Tell me to talk to you about Descartes. You'll want me to show you I can recite the elegies of the "white fathers" you so sorely adore. If I pass your tests, you'll give me more tests. You'll absorb my kaleidoscopic flavors and red splashes, you'll sink into my sway. I'll become your "ethnic" subject, you'll win a grant off of me. Wepa!

So go ahead. Snatch my sorpresas, blunt my swinging song. Take nibbles from my silhouette.

You just don't know, oh you don't know. While you're gobbling me, fitting me into your common jaw, I'm a knife. I'm a clawed weapon, ripping, ramming through the boxes you try to fit over my raging skull.

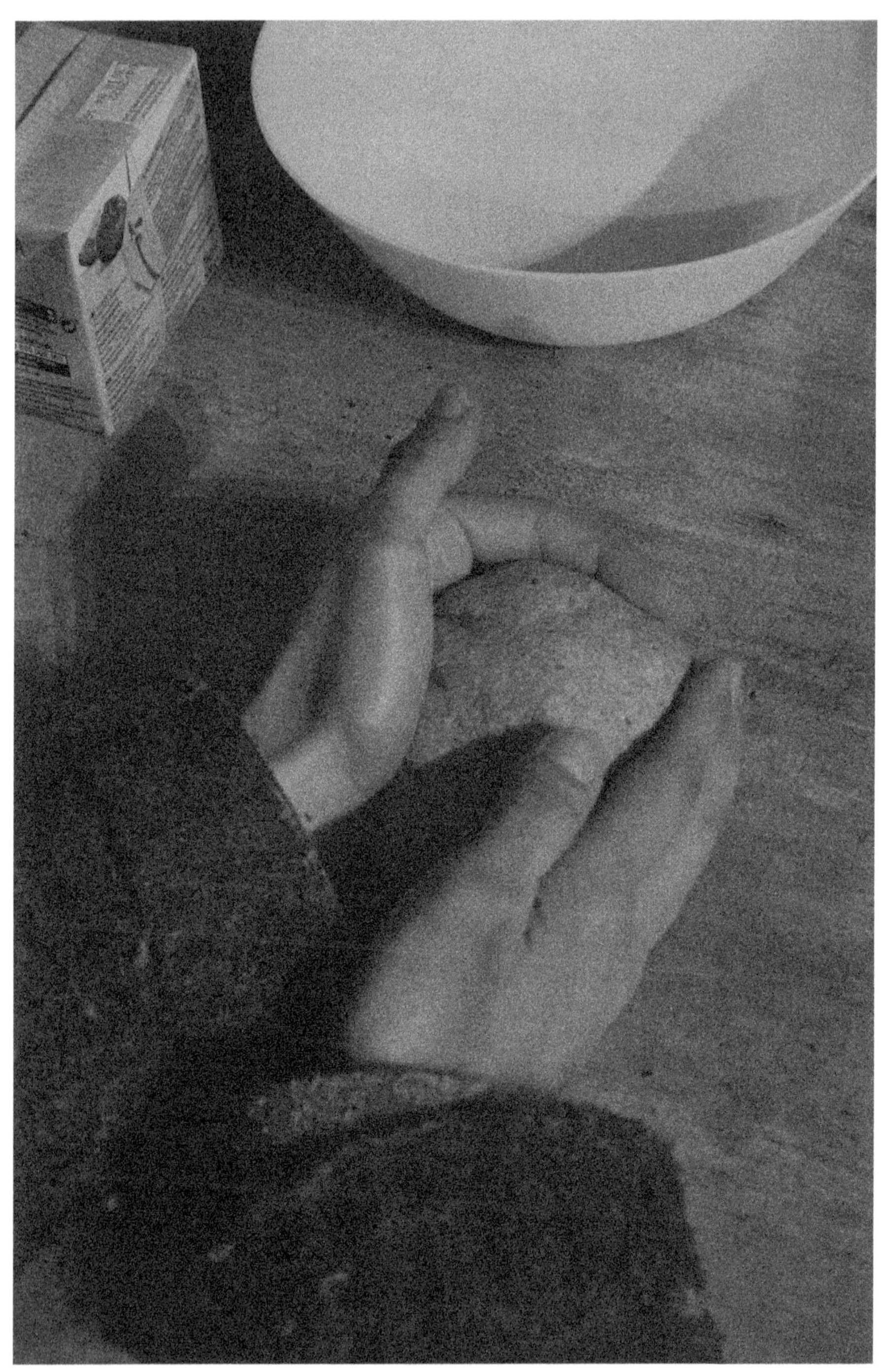

Untitled by Pablo Marcos

a celebration of masa

by Anyély Gómez-Dickerson

---

no, not that masa

we ain't cooking tamales, we celebrating

esa masa that wiggles & giggles

that masa shaking up & down

& all around my masa hips & stacked

on my well-stacked masa everything

that bountiful masa not meant to be harvested

as it strains from these way-too-thin bra straps

& everywhere masaness is bursting from my masa

seams & who cares if my masa ain't Victoria-approved

that bitch can shove her Secret

where her masa don't shine

cuz we're here ¡presente! & showing up

for this womanhood party so bold & pronounced

from a place of power & joy we hip hop, salsa & bounce

cuz this masa never meant to elicit nasty catcalls or warrant

vicious slut slurs from dejected egos, this is a masa strong

in itself viviendo esa vida loca, secure in its swagger & sway

esa masa made for no one belonging to none

cuz the landscape of my masa has a population of one

proprietor: me

& assured in my ancestral masa i own it

loud & proud in my inherited masa i protect it

dancing in this masa splendor i love & celebrate it

if only for me, if only for us, if only for them

who no longer can cuz we ain't cooking tamales

with this masa today

Boy

by Jennifer Maritza McCauley

I want to lust hot like a boy. Watch me.

Set to pounce, I want to sashay and swivel behind you in an alleyway while you toss your neck my way. I want to say gimme gimme that half-smile boy, sneakily, like that coil-ed girl from the MJ video. I'm a girl, woman, little. But I'll be wearing that black jacket and you'll still be tall as bullet. And I'll be crooning your name like it's something I own but could never release.

Look. I'm going to pursue you and nobody will say that's off limits for ladies and blahety-blah-blah, so, Papi, here. Look. You cross the room, gimme them dart-sharp, flame-fire eyes and I hear you say all the things I expect you to say and I'll say what I will and fuck it. Let's call what we do something like modern-ed love.

that (sweet)song of cassava hips

by Anyély Gómez-Dickerson

---

when your cassava hips wanna dance

to your (drum)beaten   (sweet)song let 'em shake

let 'em sway & survive those trying to steal

your sweetness to spread you on toast like mango jam

just to spit you out so ignorant of your worth & your flavors

so when your cassava hips wanna dance

to your loud (drum)beaten (sweet)song let 'em salsa & hip hop

because yours is a radiance, a sweetness & a swagger

that will not be snuffed out   never again stolen

cuz you are the beauty & the bruja with that (sweet)song

you are more than cassava hips

you are (deep)oceans & (freed)fists

you are the broken chains of ancestors & the (sweet)song

of freedom so when your cassava hips wanna dance

that eternal (drum)beaten (sweet)song

dance cuz you are of soil & sand & primordial dust

& that (secret)eternal cassava dancer

so when your cassava hips scream to move

to that (forbidden)rhythm across this land let 'em

rumba with riotous pride & walk past all those jealous

of your (drum)beaten (sweet)song

all those trying to silence that (sweet)syncopation

of your cassava hips de esas caderas always swaying

always (rule)breaking into new tomorrows

with dreams paved by your joy, you strength

& your yesterdays cuz you make your own

(drum)beaten (sweet)song because

you are the (sweet)song

Mountains of Underwear by Sophie Mulgrew

RE: Sugar Babe Branding

by Dylana Wagorn

Dear Marigold Barrigada,

This is my formal request to be an ambassador for your brand. I'd like some outfits for my Instagram shoots. Good outfits. Not whatever it was you sent Cindy Vande-Hei-Louis. I want the premium or whatever you call it. Like, the good stuff. We're talking about leopard print cardigans, dark red burgundy berets – I mean, like, wine red - and rhinestones on the ass of the tightest leggings, and absolutely niche graphic crop tops, and maybe a neon pink dog collar too, while we're at it.

We're talking big eggplant-sweat emoji energy over here, okay? Don't even think about bringing me anything less. I mean, it's like, in your best interest of course. If you know you know.

Anyway, Siri told me to tell you what my strengths are and what I can bring to your brand's reputation, but I think that's a bad idea. Instead, I've sent you my entire history of influencer stardom narrated by yours truly in an mp4 file – using a very neat trick where the email thingy lets you, like, digitally paperclip files to an email (it took me forever to figure that, why did they make it so needlessly difficult? I don't understand! MAKE IT MAKE SENSE.)

I'm sure what I've got there is just gonna blow you away, so make sure you've got your tits glued on tight because they are about get knocked off, mm'kay? But while I'm already here I just wanted to let you know that while you're getting booed for your recent avant-garde line, I'm over here cheering for ya babe. I really love your "Basking in the Glow" spring series – no matter what anyone says. Like, I wear your "Bensen Jetspeed" purse every day. It's so glam, and I mean that from the bottom of my stone-cold bitchy heart.

Toodles,

Sugar B. Berries

Untitled by Reba Spike

Guy on Hinge

by Madison Whatley

Said, *I didn't think anyone actually lived here*, meaning Miami, but I do. My great-grandparents are buried in Hialeah and will sink with this state, and maybe, so will I. The little flowers broke off my new heels while making out with this stupid-ass from New Jersey on South Beach, and while I loved his abs, I thought I left kissing under the guard shack behind in high school, and sand kept hitting my face. Sometimes I think about how everything that has made me will become ocean soon. I think about it every time I sunbathe. It relaxes me to close my eyes, listen, and think about the waves rising over me. Maybe I'm meant to lay to rest on the seabed. My aunt says in another life I probably died on the Titanic because I get an urge to look up photos of the wreckage late at night, even though they scare me. I'm not sure I want myself or my family to belong to the Atlantic, but there's no choice. I live next to a tomb. The guy from Hinge asked me what kind of adventure I'm looking for on the app. It's a stupid question, so I said I want to get bit by a shark. He said he didn't expect that answer. One day, when Miami is underwater, I hope a shark moves into my apartment. The shark wouldn't have to pay rent or marry someone to split bills with. I hope she finds the flowers from my heels and clips them in her gills to go on dates. If she went on my Hinge date, she'd say, *Thank you for the Jack and Cokes, but you have a weird tongue.* I wouldn't want to bother the shark. I just want a small love bite from something that could kill me.

Pretty Great White by Michelle K. Robinson

Self Portrait as a Great White

by Terin Weinberg

"Very few [Great White Shark] females have ever been studied, and
reports suggest as few as 10 have been dissected. Not many are held
captive and when they are, they're not quiet about it." -OCEANA

My dorsal gleans
the current
as I torpedo
      & breach
the surface to catch
a mouthful
of nothing.

Eyes rolled back
      all my whites
showing; they never
      close. I'm not
built for it.
      My chromatophores
shift before I take

a bite of fresh air.
      Charcoal—dust
grey—white bellied

& camouflaged
      from you. My body
reverberates its mass

back down, beneath.
      Who knows
how far
      I'll go to feed.

Friendship

by Jennifer Maritza McCauley

Hey, there. Pal.

*

I remember when I could see the loveliness in your teeth. Wedged, full and waiting, plump with kindness.

*

You message me and say "thanks, friend" and it sounds sharp-hearted. You don't feel that way. You think you are being kind. There was a day desire sizzled hot-red and we were never chums nor fast buddies.

When you see me now you see a plain woman, someone you can no longer love. You've lost all desire so quickly? How is that possible? What do I not know? I don't care to know. Baby, these wings bursting from backblades never tire.

*

When desire is born, expect the infantile. Bucking and elbowing, children leading children, children chiding children, adult bodies with baby blood. We're clawing for the quickest kick, expecting nothing less than tantrum.

Desire, love, feels like a miracle but it's really just the phenomenon of finding your face in someone else.

Dear friend, I can't see your face anymore. So go on.

Somewhere in the Swamp, 1961

by Terin Weinberg

"During the Cold War, the United States military placed at least
eight nuclear weapons permanently...the Department of Defense
calls "broken arrows"—America's stray nukes" –Erick Sass

The Carolina farmland is held by bodies
      of unsung war. The swamp nearby
      sifts & bubbles on hot days
      & the plane's belly shifts, slides
deeper into the earth. She's hiding her
      broken arrows, deciding
      if they ever should be found.
North Carolina farmland holds the carcass
of a B-52 that misfired
      & crashed off the airbase
      into the winter's morning.
In her belly, two weapons wait
      to be found in the swampland.
      The government forbids
      looking for them, so they
      wait through the seasons,
shifting in the muck. The plane stomach
      holds twenty-four megatons
      of nuclear energy, rolling
      near her ribcage, in the murk.
In the Carolina dirt, nuclear bombs sleep.

Don't Drink The Blackout (2) by Halsey Hyer

Lying

by Jennifer Maritza McCauley

It's time for the ultrasound
And the technician seeks
To check my heart.

I'm tied up to ribboning wire,
Gelled electrodes grasp my
Chest-skin.

Do you have anxiety? Or something else?
He asks immediately
As his eyes roam the screen,
Yes, I tell him. I do. And Something Else.

I'm surprised he can tell,
I thought I was able to mask
it, stuff it fiercely inside until faux
calm slips out.

Apparently my heart doesn't lie.

You get up from your chair
And stroke me gently,

Keep doing that, the technician
Tells you. Yes, that's right
Now her heart rate is perfect.

I sink into your nested warmth,
Your fingertips
Speak baby
lullabies to my twisted arm.

Tender you, you give me
sacred rest, with you.

Wren & Blayze by Kaitlyn Whatley

Triptych: The Evolution of My Ass

by Kristin Marie

My ass at 25
at the Venetian pool
captured on film
posted on the internet
for others' pleasure
misguided act of empowerment

My ass at 35
locked down
in an attempt at self-love
taken off the internet
because I saw cellulite
a bout of self-loathing

My ass at 40
thicker than ever
my body's cushion
for your eyes only
it starts with
acceptance

Othered Anatomy

by Terin Weinberg

I'm just a windpipe/waiting to swallow/ready to curl back/my tongue/
& fill my throat//I'm the lung/cavity filling/with breath/releasing/pent up/
air. The nasal cavity/expands//becomes/me/I'm the ribcage/shuffling
along/with the spinal cord/My bones//are shifting/with the sway/of the
skeleton//I'm the metatarsals/arching the foot/of this body/with every step
forward//If you ever see/my brain/in a jar/please still tell me/I'm beautiful/

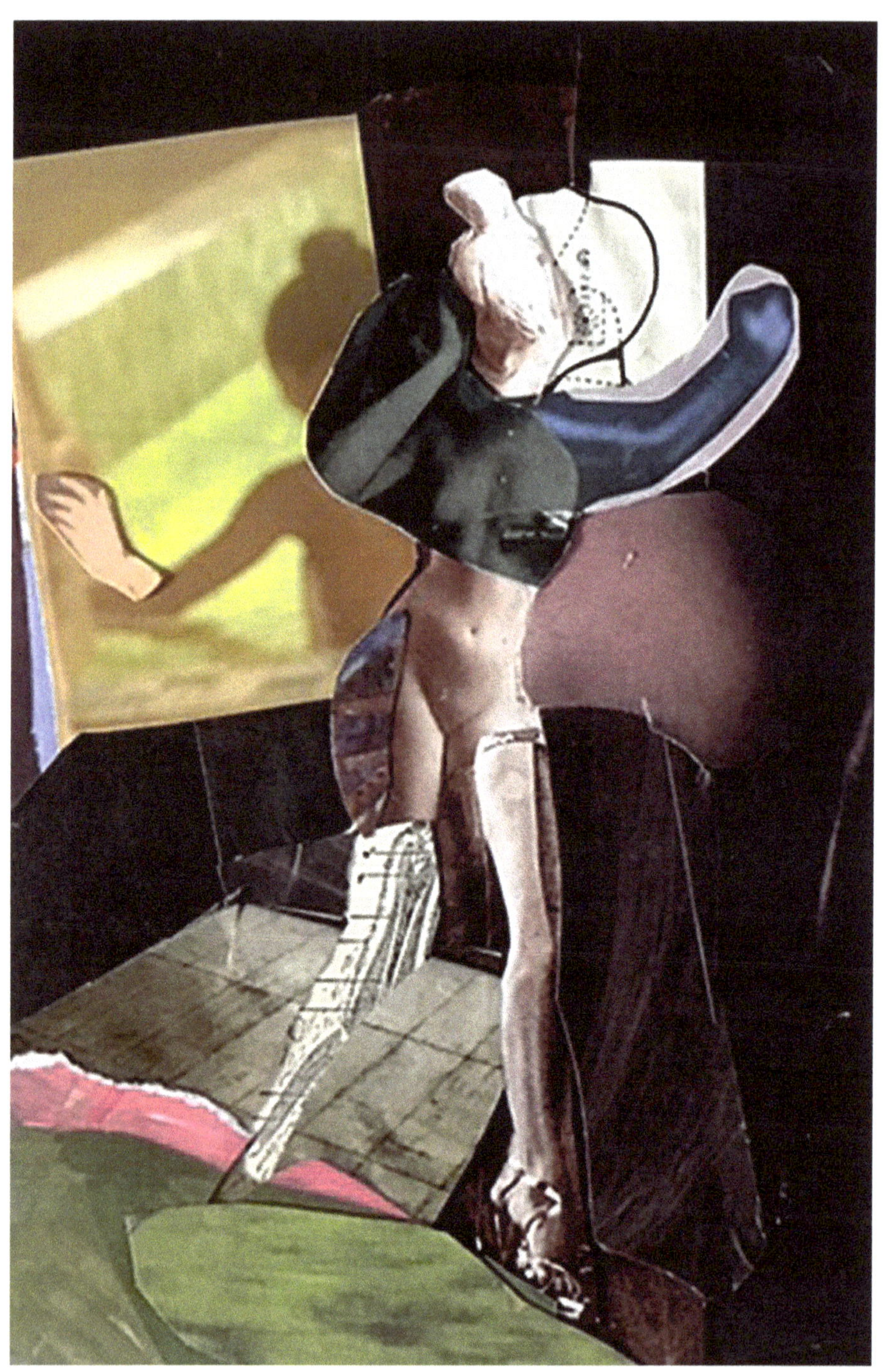

Object Lesson ii by Kathy Bruce

Ghazal on Learning to Love My Stomach

by Kristin Marie

To get me to sleep, my mother used to breastfeed me. Lullaby stomach.
The doctor measured how I thrived by the size of my head, my limbs, my stomach.

My sisters and I used to dance around the living room singing Whitney Houston songs,
dressed in matching ruffled underwear. I never thought to hate my stomach.

The paramedics filled it with charcoal after I swallowed hundreds of aspirin
when I didn't know how to love any part of me, let alone my junior-high stomach.

When I was eighteen my grandmother screamed at me *You'll never find a husband*
after she spotted the orange and yellow tattoo of the sun on my stomach.

Tanning, sit-ups, yoga, diets, shapewear, and all types of torture to obtain
the flat, toned abdomen I could be proud to call my Fourth of July stomach.

A tape measure to chart my shrinking progress. Why do I love my body parts
only when they start to disappear? My arms, my hips, my thighs, my stomach.

I used to drink three or four glasses of wine then try to fill the emptiness
by drunk dialing a man who would come by and come on my stomach.

Kristin, you have a stomach—a muscular, miraculous, hollow organ that makes
its own juice to keep you alive. Practice saying this: I love, I love, I love my stomach.

Drunk on His Gaze by Sophie M. Mulgrew

The Speech

by Marianna Faynshteyn

The bridesmaids stood alongside a projector, looking out to the wedding guests who peered back at them as though they were flight attendants about to give safety instructions. Nat, the maid of honor, signaled to the DJ, and the main theme from "Once Upon a Time in America" started playing. The guests hadn't even stopped eating–at least the old relatives hadn't–chewing with their mouths open while locking eyes with the women. Nat heard someone whisper, "Is this from the Godfather?" She swallowed her disappointment. The song from The Godfather had been her first choice, but the other girls thought it was "too Italian." Nat looked at Jane, Irina, and Vicky, standing behind the microphone in their identical dresses and similar hairstyles, and when squinting hard enough, their similar faces, too. They looked like a girl group, Nat thought—the *Girls from the Shtetl,* or maybe, *The Esthers.*

"Ready?" Irina asked Nat. The melancholic song was supposed to be a joke, something cheeky but nostalgia-inducing, a backdrop to the shtick they had come up with, but now it just seemed sad.

"Nat?" Vicky asked, more concerned than Irina.
Nat pressed the remote, and an image appeared on the wall beside them.
"Awwwww," the wedding guests all said, all at once, the sound elongated and even toned, like air seeping out of a balloon.

It was a grainy photo of a family of four, a young boy in dungarees and a baby in a faded onesie, the father mustachioed and tired-looking, and the mother a 90s copy of Sonya, a beautiful blonde with a head full of teased hair.

"In 1992, Sonya and her family," Jane said, "came from Minsk to Brooklyn, quite happily. Of course Mama Inna and Papa Fima had shed many tears, but to give their kids a better life, they were willing to sacrifice their home and careers." It was the beginning of a story they had all heard, because they all had the same one. Even the girls' parent's names weren't that much different. "I don't understand why we couldn't just tell a funny story," Jane had complained when they had been discussing speech ideas. Nat didn't explain that it had been Sonya's explicit wish to have something like this. "A montage of old photos, you know," Sonya told her, "something cinematic." As her maid of honor, Nat had felt obligated to make this happen, as though she were granting wishes to a dying child.

Another photo popped up: little Sonya with pigtails and a lunchbox standing in front of the door of her family's apartment building.

"When Sonya was ready to go to *sadik*, she had caused a lot of havoc. Instead of getting her shots for school, she ran away from the doctor's office like a little fool." Naturally, they didn't have a photo that captured this event, the image of her eventual first day of school the closest they could manage, but it was a legendary story, one that demonstrated sweet Sonya's occasional boldness and activated her lifelong fear of needles.

"Who knew Sonya was an anti-vaxxer!" A man yelled, to which half of the crowd laughed and the other sat confused.

More photos appeared, Sonya growing older, standing on her own, always smiling while her brother looked displeased, her parents weary, her mother's hair becoming shorter, her father's thinner. What a beautiful child, blessed with dimples, round cheeks and the brightest eyes–but also something else. Sonya looked like happiness came easy to her. Surrounded by her family members who could only make attempts at ease, Sonya appeared alongside them, simply happy. Perhaps this had been the gift of just barely being born somewhere else. She had been carried across borders in a protective casing, shielded away from the kind of pain and humiliation everyone else who understood "before" and "after" had to endure. And maybe only these guests would notice it, the preciousness that enveloped Sonya. Nat looked over at the guests and saw faces that recognized something beyond the bride and her family. They saw themselves–they were looking at Sonya's memories but imagining their own, placing their faces onto the ones projected in front of them, their expressions screwed up, smiling but ready to cry. Was there a Russian word for this? This wistfulness, this cut between pain and happiness? For sure something in Yiddish, Nat thought.

They had transitioned to Irina's section, Sonya's early adolescence.

"We all know Sonya for her skilled dancing and her great costumes," Irina said, a photo of little Sonya in a red sequined ensemble, covering her as much as a bathing suit would, a face flanked with bright makeup, "and all that presence that could only be described as va-va-voom." Nat looked through the crowd to spot Sonya through the howls of laughter. *Va va voom?* She thought. How had they all agreed to that?

"Where's Sonya?" Nat whispered to Vicky.

Vicky remained looking straight ahead, at the crowd, preserving a commitment to their act. "The sweetheart table," she whispered.
The sweetheart table, with her sweetheart, of course, separated from everyone else. Nat turned in the direction of the table, of the sweethearts, in the direction she had remembered it being, but somehow the sweethearts had been swallowed up by the

surroundings. Nat felt the hall had become smaller, encased in a web of memories, like dozens of Russian spiders had crawled from their chairs and linked their individual memory webs to one another.

"And one fateful day, she met the friends she'd know her whole life," Irina said, louder and with more enthusiasm, a photo of the five of them together, in a collection of bright colored t-shirts, their teeth lined with braces, "the ones who'd be her bridesmaids on the day she'd become Paul's wife." The crowd's tender noises became louder, almost uncontained. There they were, the five of them, at the height of their friendship, at a time when the hours they were separated were fewer than the hours spent together. Nat could feel something catching in her throat, as though something were being exhumed out of her. Her eyes fogged with tears. She realized the montage featured no more photos of all of them together. And there was Sonya, on one of the ends, but still somehow the center, with her wide-faced smile and bright eyes, her preciousness, her protective casing, still intact.

"I can't see Sonya," Nat whispered again to Vicky, her voice trembling.

Vicky turned to Nat annoyed, until she saw Nat's face. "What's wrong?" She asked. Just then, Irina handed Vicky the mic. Vicky squeezed Nat's hand before turning to the guests.

"Sonya has always been a beauty who liked to experiment with her look," Vicky said and a second later a projected teenage Sonya appeared, her hair slicked back into a bun, ears adorned with hoop earrings and her lips lined in an exaggerated color. And then the photo widened out to show the full image, a brutish looking boy in a sweatshirt and spiky hair appearing next to Sonya. "But her poor taste in boys, thank god she shook!" The crowd laughed like it had been the funniest thing–isn't being a pretty girl with wolves for boys to choose from a hoot? In the photo, Sonya had a different smile, her lips tight and somewhat pulled up, like a clothesline that sagged in the middle. It looked practiced and dulled, dimples and teeth missing and the shine in her eyes gone. How had Nat not noticed it until now? This must be what it's like to be a clueless parent, even though, eventually, Nat had found out what had happened—a date with a "nice" boy that didn't end nicely. And maybe because it felt so commonplace and maybe because Nat found out about it well after it had happened, after she could do anything about it, Nat never thought–never wanted to think–that it had changed Sonya, that it altered her so deeply that it was visible.

"Nat," Vicky said, placing the microphone in Nat's hand.
Nat held the microphone in her hand, the melancholic song playing on a loop in the background. A photo of Sonya and Paul flashed behind her. The guests clasped their hands as though overcome at the sight. There they were, the bride and groom, back when they were first a couple, sitting at a table in a picturesque garden, their newness and excitement jumping off their faces.

Vicky put her hand on Nat's shoulder and leaned into her ear. "This is your section, remember?"

Yes, she thought. Of course she remembered. She was the Maid of Honor. She should regale the guests with the story of Sonya and Paul, even though there wasn't much of a story. Paul had always been there, waiting in the wings, waiting for Sonya to notice him. And eventually, Sonya had. Happily ever after. Nat looked behind her, zoning in on Sonya's face. A version of her smile had returned, though a sadness sat in her eyes. The photo changed, another photo of Sonya and Paul appeared.

Vicky gingerly removed the microphone from Nat's hand. "Let me," she said, her concerned eyes locking with Nat's until she turned to the guests.

"Sonya and Paul had met as children," Vicky said, pausing, perhaps to the guests it seemed for dramatic effect, "and once Sonya was done with the bad boys, Paul set in motion the plan he had had since he was ten," she said. "He wined and dined her, put her on a pedestal and made her a queen, and proposed with a ring that was almost obscene!"

A new photo emerged, the day Sonya and Paul had become engaged. It could have been a stock photo, the positioning so standard: Paul on his knee as Sonya knelt over covering her face, the Eiffel Tower in the background. The guests cheered, captivated now as though these details were new to them, as though not every single one of them had liked it on Facebook. "A fairytale!" A comment had read. But had Sonya really wanted it like that? Had she wanted to be like thousands of women who had been proposed to in front of a tourist sight, surrounded by throngs of strangers?

Nat faced the guests completely for the first time. Looking at them suddenly felt like looking at ghosts, at familiar strangers she had no real relationship with. An overwhelming self-awareness crept over her and made everything feel like a performance. This couldn't be real life, this has to be someone else's design done in the styling of life-like. How else could someone explain the costumes they were wearing? The rehearsed words they were saying? The fact that Sonya was marrying Paul? Nat was standing on the outside of it all now, Vicky's words sounding muffled and garbled to her, as though she spoke them into a glass bottle. Once you know it's all an act, how can you go on acting? Nat reached for the microphone, snatching it out of Vicky's hands.

"Uh oh!" The same man from before yelled in the style of rapper Lil' Jon.

The girls looked at Nat with concern as the crowd laughed. Nat made a wave with her hand, *it's ok* even though she wasn't sure.

"Sonya is a very special person," Nat said and then turned to point at Sonya in the photo projected behind her, remembering the performance. "And, Paul," she started, trying to find the words, "he's a good guy."

"Aww Paul!" The man shouted.

"Who the fuck keeps doing that?!" Nat snapped back, as low "oohs" and shrill "oys" of the guests bounced off each other, sounding like a Yiddish edition of a tacky talk show. All these stupid boys, she thought. "Why do you have to be like that?" She asked. "You're ruining it! Sonya deserves," her voice cracked. Now everyone and everything was still. Nat looked down, away from the crowd, the girls, the background of the happy couple. If only she could cut around the circumference, around her feet, like a cartoon character with a saw, and drop down into another lair. She held her hand to her face and started crying. And she knew, it was the kind of crying that dislodged and unmoored, not just like a storm, like an act of God, pulling everything down.

LOBOTOMY!

by m. v. riasanovsky

give me the sluttiest
      lobotomy you have please

                        is it queering the space when
              i steal allergy medication from the
              grocery store

when willow is in love with xander for
      like four seasons of buffy or whatever
         and later falls in love with a beautiful witch
            who has the softest voice and
                she comes out as a lesbian
                  i felt that

                      listen i don't ask for corporate
              sponsorships they just come to me
okay? i fucking love my brands !!!!!!!!!!!!!
          i love fucking my brands !!!!!!!!
      i love fucking the moons sweat and the
      dirtiest nastiest comets in the sky

i did weird sick shit for men on manyvids before
         onlyfans was even conceptualized
          it was disgusting and beautiful art
       people ask about my photography portfolio
         but my old external hard drive crashed
     so none of the time lapse stars melting into one another
or the delicate flowers and trees across southeastern virginia
or the colorful midnight photoshoots with my gorgeous spontaneous lovely friends all of
              that is lost in some celestial cyberspace

i just have the stuff you'd need to pay me to see sorry

is it queering the space when i am
            entranced by the silence in between my
                        own heartbeats
            or in the planned parenthood
                        the silence before the shot to my leg
how many waiting rooms have i queered up
cathedrals and magically revered spaceships
            linear time, sacred time, call it what you want
                        watching the top ten jersey shore fights with you
                        at the planned parenthood

                                        there's always enough
                        if you look deeply through the telescope
            what you're seeking is delicious
                        and covered in caramel and
            old wires

there's a squirrel running on the roof
            covered in caramel and old wires
                        quick call the dawn soap commercial people
                        they love cleaning oily birds or whatever squirrels are

                                    just be gentle when you reach
                        your hand into the menacing core
                        the bowels the cavern i had that bad memory in
            let's talk about something else actually

look, i'm not saying it's part of
            the anomalies or the ritual
                        i'm just saying i can't park
                        but parallel
            ya i'm good at that

                                                listen breathe wait listen okay
                             listen breathe feel the sting under your skin, the
                      pinch when the needle hits your leg
                          delicate goosebumps crawling up shhhh

shhhh
      it's okay
           you're safe

                                                  collapsable radiation filtered
                            through nebulous heartsong filling the brim
                    of the dark in my eyelids when i close them and hold my
          breath and they dance twinkle lightbeam along the creamy smoothness of
your eyes kinder egg coded that's fucking nasty but it had to be said

i don't know anything but i often
          answer questions assertively
               even when i'm wrong like
                    i knew the answer
but i didn't
i didn't know
i didn't know you'd queer elsewhere

xo confessional

by m. v. riasanovsky

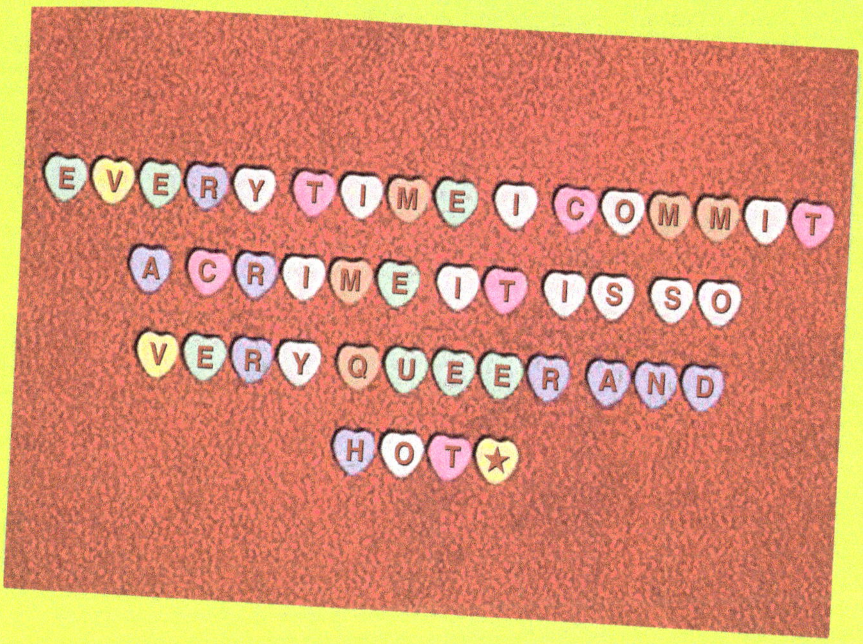

Rooms

by Moriah Brown

Virginia says every woman needs a
room— I think of my room in Texas filled
with books and paint
art of the places I wanted to go and pothos plants,
a room of blissful childhood dreaming
the world was distant still
the room I learned the beauty
of solitude and its ache too
the room where I became me.

I think of my room in New York
the one I sit in now
all mine, safe from the chaos of my days
it still has books and it has the scribbled
notes of the truths I try to write into beauty
it has faces of the artists I respect
those people who persisted like I want to—
This room too has plants
most of them half dead but still pressing on
and this room also has a desk
a desk to get lost in and enter into other worlds
a portal here in my own apartment—

This is the room where I learned to be me.

These two tiny words—be me—
laughable
they don't represent the magnitude of the meaning—
Some days I fight tooth and nail to
be me
and some days it's easy like sliding into a silk
robe, so easy to
be me
but wherever I am
it's always the room
the room with my books and my words and my tears
it's always the room that lets me be.

Clean The Table by Mulgrew

Object Lesson Kathy Bruce

HIP

by Terri Watrous Berry

These hips have rocked
men and babies all
night long, given a
toe-hold to teethers
and measure to a man.
These hips have locked
hearts and souls
and stole daddios whole.

Bimbo Tingo

by Sharlyn Page

Under the gumbo limbo with its
blush and peel
I took the present opportunity
to cop a feel
your skirt was silk and silk
between my fingers in a gliding dream

Leaves drop like scarce confetti
drifting to ground
your lazy hair spread akimbo
accompanies the gasping sound
life held intoxicant,
an interstice of breath
reared up rose-red and rampant,
the plush and perfect,
antidote to death

Diablerie

by Sharlyn Page

French in concept
the rolled half
swallowed 'r',
freewheeling sexuality
topless beaches
slim eaters
of croissants
tiny espressos
express the negligence
of makeup
the negligees
of silk
and subdued
manicures,
wine for lunch
with naps in rooms,
blinds drawn for yellow
lit leg spread
ambiance,
and too high up the
rococo facade
for passersby
to hear the ecstasy,
skill, – and taunt –
you can't be French
just because you want.

The Other Cousin

by Nona Lea

Call me the Other Cousin—
Cousin Its Cousin It,
the redheaded regional Addams family variant
irking Meri wool threads from every goose flesh orifice
from head to heels I cascade gendered:

to be / not, & not, / to be

vavavooming with secondary sex organs:
gobbledygook, tee-ha-ha-ha-ha,
and that yokai the cat choked out
sashaying head to toes with saliva
across the ambiguously beige carpet
giving an owlish wink /

My preferred pronouns are you there /
Vans shoes / crotch goblin / or Lord of the Cheese /
anything but Elmo /

I raggedy anne in a room
hairy and undefinable /

My sheep dog shimmy makes
everyone's li-bi-toes pop off
and toodaloo to sell themselves at Trader Joe's,
organic and scoopable /

Little do their button eyes know,
I am ooo-la-la generous,
dropping red threads in shopping baskets
squirming alphabets
goodbye seahorse mommy /

I populate this hanging orb with my folklore;

who run the sewers red
set azaleas ablaze
hitch a ride into houses
and dna themselves in a soup bowl or two /

Inside others those wicked little fibers
noodle themselves little cloth dolls,
synthing red in darkness, whispering
mistranslations from the holy /

migrating through the bloodstream
filling every vein with cobwebs
spindling around the brain
fuzzy cocoons full of questioning voodoo
years from now hatching from fleshy loop eyes
a red hair or two, growing another cousin

inside each and every one of you.

Advice from Yeast
after Amy Gerstler's Advice from a Caterpillar

by Elizabeth Kandall

Jiggle your way into an expanse.
Dissolve, shutter, divide, shutter, divide again,
Entitlement be yours! Float on the current
eat sugars, spread out. Be a simple creature, bubble
foam, become yourself in double volume. Get too big
to contain yourself, stretch, stumble, reproduce rapidly,
bud new cells, pinch your middle, make daughters. Let
them come loose, wear bud scars where they left you. There
may be long times when dry, inactive you stay packaged. Don't
take it personally when they call you a stress granule. Rehydrate
get mixed up with all kinds, ferment. Push your way, let your heat
swell and lift you. When they ask for proof, even though
they ask no other food for this, show them, be severe
persevere, give them proof. Die and keep going.

****the heat death of the planet****

by m. v. riasanovsky

****the heat death of the planet****
****being queer for a little while****
****the ice death of the (under)known universe****

we already know this - time is our insistence of personal significance
can you understand yourself through entropy, our clumsy entanglement in perpetual
disordering
we already know this - beyond a few feet of distance, time is not consistent regular or static
can you untwine belonging and possession   *   *   *   *   *
                        fear and exploitation   *   *   *   *   * *
        *   *   anger and rage   *   *   *   *   * *
                                            the illusion of time and urgently needed
                            revolution
        *   *   *   *   *
        *   *   *   *   i ask you this i ask myself i ask again

****

postmodern relational theory: the edges of self and other are blurrier than we think
my conceptual projection of 'yesterday' (aka yesterday): you're playing a multiplayer
online video game;
someone has their mic on and a baby laughs in the background

****

the poems of environmentalist parents on the anthropocene extinction are weird
because they still give genders to their babies, who are the locus of their anti-natalist
concerns
i cannot get past this when i'm reading about the inevitability of our end-times

****

two years ago
                i hold hands with two queer people at once at the kink party
two years before
                i make out with two straight people at once at the tennis party

****

we already know this - black holes are not an absence
their characteristic 'event horizon' fits nicely with our false illusions of time and nothing-
ness, however, they are really quite expansive
i hate the phrase 'gender-neutral' and its implication of lack, its dis-recognition
we are quite expansive, indeed

****

        i used to eat polly pocket shoes now i'm a queer nonbinary lesbian

****

your hair is soft even when you
      are too tired to shower
           i have known and loved your softness
          in the valley of mountains that
              will be merely lost memories
             of long-forgotten hills
      once this planet is laid to rest

****

what is   aDeath   but a becoming
what is   time   but the earnest reaction to this
untouchable vastness
what is   grief   but the natural bend to a con-
sciousness of entropy

****

the universe is chaotic and queer *   * *   * *   *   * *
polyamorous and perhaps stringy or loopy or both *   * * * * ** *
who really is to say   *   *   * *   *   *   *   *

****

i endorse queer-coded villains in fiction
&&&& maybe someday i will 'replace' my hormones once more
&&&& maybe someday i will watch the twilight of this rebellious
season unfold
crawl towards liberation wherever i am welcomed to, wherever i am useful
bask in the light and divinity of queer sensuality
make movement towards those victories that i can in this supposed lifetime

fight forest fires
invite anarchic upheaval without hesitation
spit in someone's mouth   with love   as adornment

see what happens next

Online

by Jennifer Maritza McCauley

MidnightWanderer477: Hey

MidnightWanderer477: Hi!! I just wanted to introduce myself. I'm Midnight and I've been reading the shounen and shojo parodies on your site every week. The gundam wing one was SO FUNNY. Hiro's hair is really spikey...you're right!

MidnightWanderer477: Hey

PlanetSenshi191: U really reading it?

MidnightWanderer477: YES

PlanetSenshi191: Nice

MidnightWanderer477: Thanks for responding! Your site is very cool.

PlanetSenshi191: Thanks, you. I'm glad someone cares.

MidnightWanderer477: What do you mean?

PlanetSenshi191: The trolls got to it and I was planning to just shut it down tomorrow.

MidnightWanderer477: OH NO

PlanetSenshi191: Yeah

MidnightWanderer477: Please don't. PLEASE

PlanetSenshi191: I dunno. I'm still thinking about it. I'm not very popular at my school already so I don't want to get my self esteem gutted everyday.

MidnightWanderer477: PLEASE keep it up. I'm not popular either. In fact my Dad's never around and my mom is always fighting with him and I look forward to your parodies every week to get me through stuff and and

MidnightWanderer477: HELLO

MidnightWanderer477: Sorry if I shared too much!!

PlanetSenshi191: No. I feel like you. Stop saying sorry. Be like Sailor Jupiter, always tough and ready to fight. "I'll make you feel so much regret, it'll leave you numb! I am the Pretty Guardian who fights for Love and Courage!"

MidnightWanderer477: I bet you're really cool in real life!

PlanetSenshi191: I am but only in my own head. Everyone at my school thinks I'm a loser

MidnightWanderer477: Mine too. But at least we can connect here!

PlanetSenshi191: Yeah

MidnightWanderer477: What will your next parody be?

Planet Senshi191: Dunno. What u think I should do? I did too many sailor moons and yu yu hakushos

MidnightWanderer477: Maybe Revolutionary Girl Utena! Because Utena is going to become a prince herself! That's what we can do!! Become princes ourselves!!

PlanetSenshi191: OK. I'll do it

MidnightWanderer477: Yay! YAY!!

PlanetSenshi191: Only for you

Midnightwanderer477: WOOHOO

PlanetSenshi191: OK u can calm down

Midnightwanderer477: *breathes* OK OK

PlanetSenshi191: Hey

MidnightWanderer477: Yeah???

PlanetSenshi191: thxxx friend

MidnightWanderer477: ?????

PlanetSenshi191: Nm

A Play With No Plot

by Arnaldo Batista

The play opens in a desert. The wind roars, Foleyed in with the ripping of paper and a wolf howling in a long distance of at least one hundred meters. The two men, MAN 1, and MAN 2, are queer. MAN 1 sports a thick moustache and a T-Shirt that says I SUCK DICK. MAN 2 wears a leather harness and hasn't showered for a few days. Where they come from and how they got here doesn't matter. The wind roars, leaving much unsaid and even more unheard.

MAN 1: [Checking his wrist for the time, though he has no watch, a marker of something he used to once have, but has no longer] The sun…. about seven, you reckon…. have we been here

MAN 2: What did you….
    [MAN 2 walks closer to MAN 1, stumbles over a rock]
    Fuck… hurt my… damn this stings, this

MAN 1: [Sees the blood, winces, but rips the sleeve off his shirt to bandage the shin of MAN 2. This heals him.] Here…. That's a deep cut… shouldn't be walking…. it's so dark…. you said there was time

MAN 2: There's always time for…. *[He laughs at his own good joke]* But, they forgot us…. They always

MAN 1: They always forget us…. How's that…. Better? *[MAN 1 sops the blood with his ripped sleeve, applies pressure in the way he saw on General Hospital. He is in love with these things, the tenderness of treating a wound, the empathy in a slice].* … starving, could use some

MAN 2: Don't worry about it…. a scrape…. nopales over the dune *[MAN 2 points at the dune, high and blowing. How he sees nopales is a mystery. Whether or not there exists nopales past the dune is of no importance. Both MAN 1 and MAN 2 will die from exposure.]*

The play closes in the desert, the two men walking to the dune. MAN 1 holds the limping MAN 2 by the shoulder, MAN 2 depending all his weight on him, so much weight. The thing about deserts and dunes and sand is the dune will disappear, the dune is too far, the dune is in fact a mountain, in fact a crater. The dune doesn't exist, but the men walk to it anyway. The men are hungry. The men are forgotten.

PLAN A PLAN B Carolyn Schlam

Ode to My Breasts

by Salem B. Holden

Chopped / mangled / scalpel salves saves
skin, palms pressed firmly into sternum
"Welcome to manhood!"
(even though I know you're not a man)
"Well obviously you're a man"
(points to flat terrain).

I imagine my breasts now dead disintegrate
in some trashcan in Michigan
then transported trash
lying in bed with some other trash Rumpke
picked up
sitting next to silicone
and another transmasc's mangled breasts
pelicans nip at our nipples
and the construction worker yells
"Hey man, look at those titties!"

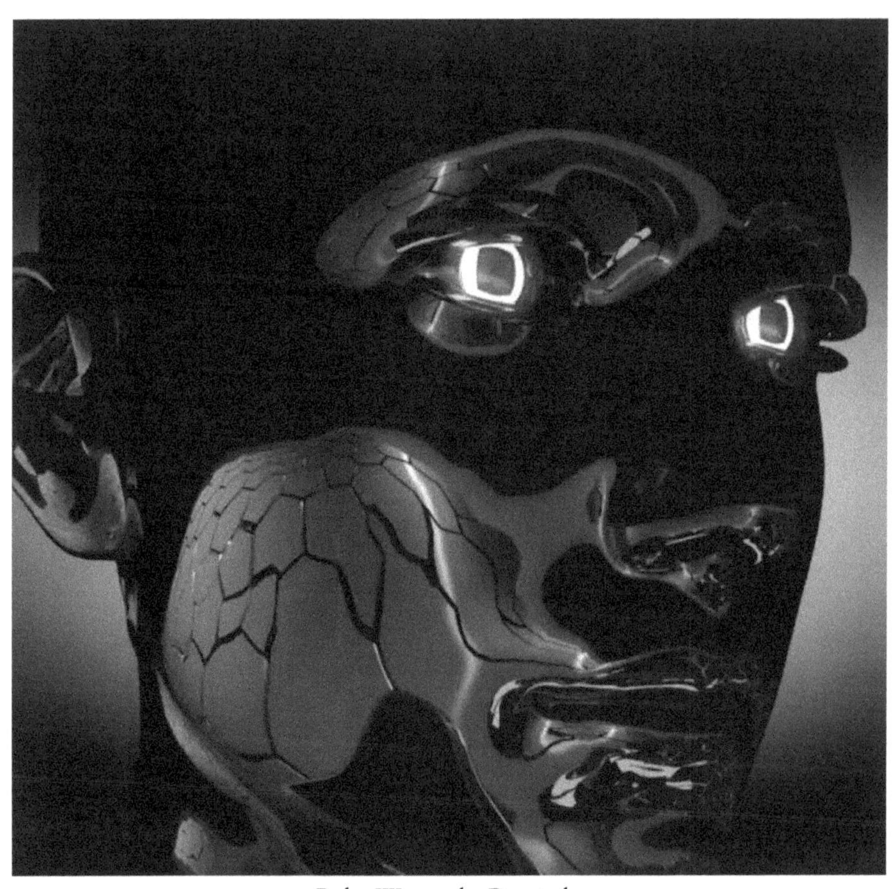

Robo Woman by Devrimb

Neon Steel

by Jennifer Maritza McCauley

She woke up in the alley, bare-fleshed and bold. Humans had this problem; flesh terrified or thrilled or enticed them into trouble, whereas Nadia knew the ramifications and beauties of skin. Which is why she chose this medium-sized body, that of a regal-dark woman with purpl'd locs and a scar on her cheek that hadn't healed after a Surgery she didn't remember. In any case, she knew she was a Black woman, fresh-feeling and Caribbean American. She knew she was first to fight, unbending and sweet-minded. She was fiery, difficult to decipher, ghosts wriggling in her head. Under the layer of brown was smooth machinery; coating her body was glistening wire; her secret in the human world, year 1987. The only possible way humans would know her Real Identity is if they caught a glimpse of her hand, wrapped in a black glove, hiding the one betrayal this body possessed. The hand was robotic, her true self. But why would strangers pull off something shadowed, a piece of her, in the first place?

The air was typical for a city that most would call cold. Dry, grit-specked, and gray, with that deadening Pittsburgh chill. Black sooted and river-streaked. Still, she smelled something scarlet, the color of a red petal. She wasn't used to smelling beauty in human alleys, but she realized she was just smelling her own perfumed body. The place around her was a'drip with brown liquids from trash heaps, and the cement was rough and mean. She stood up slowly, scanned the alley. She breathed, and the place smelled better. It smelled good, like her. A few shadows slammed open a bar door nearby, and they stopped, regarded her, glistening and gorgeous.

They approached her because of course they would. She slid past them, and when they got in close, they stopped, a bit confused themselves why they didn't try to pounce on a naked woman. They looked at each other, these drunk shadows, then they looked at her and trembled. So they passed on. She grabbed one of them as he was leaving. He threw out a hand to touch her and she gripped his fingers with her cold, robotic hand fiercely. She wrenched him back and stole his shirt; it was blue.

She threw it on, and it covered her just enough. She would have taken his pants too, but they were unattractive and dirt-grimed.

The shadows flew off and she wrenched open the door to the bar, rearranging the glove on her hand.

It was frothing with bubbling voices, as funky as feet. Fast-blinking blue and scorching pink lights draped a cloud of pulsing bodies. She pushed them all aside as she surged through the crowd. Hands reached out to grab her, and she shoved them off easily. No time to dance, though this little body loved to dance.

If she could find Dr. Cobbler this would just be done with. The whole thing was easy. Go back to before the War, kill Mr. Cobbler while he was still fucking around Pittsburgh clubs in his mid-thirties. Smooth and simple. In her world, she fought for justice, this Black Robot girl who wore human skin. She wanted a Good World in the future, and that demanded sacrifices in this former time. Therefore, one sacrifice: Dr. Cobbler deserved to die. He'd killed children, mothers, daddies, and programmed Her People, the tech-human hybrids who were constructed to aid humans, to destroy their world until it burned and simmered. She cared for humans and tech and hybrids like her but Dr. Cobbler was different. A killer deserved to be killed. The humans were always debating "an eye for an eye or a tooth for a tooth" or "do unto others as they do unto you," but she preferred to shoot a bullet through that eye or crack that tooth in half.

Speaking of guns, she unfortunately hadn't come with one, and in the process of Transportation, she'd lost her clothes and good ol Hers, her little violet rifle. So she was bare-handed, but that was OK. She'd once taken a guy out during the War with a toothpick so she'd figure it out.

What a strange place for Dr. Cobbler to be, she thought, as she scanned the joint. She saw a space at the bar, frothing with rainbow people, and sat down carefully. Men flew in, talking about fizzing drinks, and she punched them off.

"Jesus Christ. Someone had a Walk of Shame," the bartender said. He was tawny, strong-jawed but slinky. He had taut, hardened muscles that looked like they'd been shaped in the human military and smoothed out with day labor. Still, here he was getting humans hammered in here.

She blinked and winced. Human humor was stupid. "I'm just here looking for someone."

"This wouldn't be the first time I saw a girl wander in here in old clothes crying about some guy."

"I don't care about Some Guy. I'm looking for somebody specific."

"You can tell me who. I know how to keep secrets."
"Nope," she said. He half-smirked and winked. "I'm going to get you some clothes. You want something while you wait?"

"No," she said and turned to look at the crowd again. Big leaping breasts tossed around in red dresses, the drag queens on the floor stomped and stamped with shapely, flailing legs. Glitter was stretched across flashing faces.
The man called another bartender, a small balding guy, to take over and slipped out the back. She wondered why he would have random clothes on the ready in the first place, and she decided she wouldn't trust him. But she would take his clothes.

Ripe music sounded holy over thumping rhymes as folks nodded, clapped nodded. The crowd rippled as two dark-suited men slipped in, and a man with a burgundy lapel slipped upstairs to the VIP room with them. She stood up. God, if only it could be this easy. To regain the life she'd lost, to return back home to the warm arms of the only humans she loved, her Mami and Daddy. To fulfill the mission of her only friend, Maya, Dr. Cobbler's defected graduate student. Those people had raised her after she escaped from Dr. Cobbler's Tech farm. She only had to take this asshole out.

She surged forward, and the bartender tugged her back gently. She turned around, irritated. "I have something to do."

"Here, just chill the fuck out for a second," he said and gave her a folded-up pair of leggings and a pair of heels.

"Sorry about the heels. They don't look comfortable. You're so lucky my best friend is a queen who plays tonight," he said. "You guys look about the same size. And that this girl is nice. You should say thank you to her."

"OK. Thanks," she said and grabbed his leggings and heels. She stepped into the leggings, rolled them up to her knees, and tried on the heels. They were fun to wear, simple. He was right; they were her size. Why did human women love these so? She preferred bare feet but didn't want a nail to jam through her foot.

"OK, I'm just going to let you do what you do," he said.

She started toward the staircase, and he playfully tapped her back.

"You seem stuffy. Seriously. Let me get you something to drink. You look like you need water."

She ignored him. She heard him tell the other bartender he needed a few minutes, and she hoped he would leave her alone. It didn't matter anyway. She ran forward, pushing aside folks from the crowd as she slipped through shadowy spaces. Still, she felt the bartender on her heels.

"I'm Hylo," he called to her back. "What's your name? You seem like you need a friend." She could put this bitch in a headlock, but since he helped her out, she'd let him go. Plus, instinctively, he seemed harmless. If she were human, she'd think he was a little bit sexy.

Still, she didn't like having conversations while she was focused on a task. But this guy wouldn't let up. She got to the stairwell and looked up at a red rope barring her from the second level. Only two guys were guarding Dr. Cobbler. This should be fine.

Hylo lingered nearby, then loomed over her. He was really irritating at this point and needed to get out of the way.

"Please go back to your job, Hylo," she said and swung around in his direction. She bore her teeth and flapped him away.

"No," he said firmly and leaned over and smiled. "Because you're up to something. And this is my bar."

"That's sweet of you to protect it," she said and threw one gloved hand around his neck. "But you're out. Right now."

He struggled under her grip, and his eyes near bugged out. He fell to the ground, and she released him.

"Fuck, man." He got to his knees.

Her eyes widened. Now wasn't the time to give away her secret. While he was recovering, she slunk up the stairs, and this time, he accompanied her brazenly.

"Look, I'm just going to follow you. Dark/Angel Woman. Something-something, whatever your name is."

"It's Nadia," she said and dodged a man coming her way. She hated people giving her nicknames. She got to the end of the rope, and two men in black shirts who gripped drooping chests barred her from going in.

"She's with me," Hylo said over her head. "She can go through."

One of the men cocked an eyebrow. "Sorry, Hylo. She can't. There's a guest you can't see tonight."

Nadia rolled her eyes. She noticed the gun on his holster, and relief washed over her swiftly. At least she didn't have to strangle Dr. Cobbler with his own tie or something. While the man was talking to Hylo, she quickly got his gun from below the belt. She pointed it at him. Hylo kicked the other man in the stomach and also got his gun. The two men leapt forward at them, and Hylo kicked his guy down the stairs, and Nadia kneed hers in the balls and also shoved him down the stairs. This, of course, started a commotion in the club below, but Nadia's eyes were locked on Hylo, and his were locked on hers. They both drew together, at roughly the same time, and stared each other down.

"OK. Looks like you aren't the most trustworthy person," she said and winked. "Thanks for the pants."

"Never said I was trustworthy," he laughed and shook his gun. "Put yours down."

"You're protecting Dr. Cobbler? Which means you have to go too. Sorry. You seemed like you might be nice."

"You're not a criminal, Nadia," he said. "But sorry, yeah. I'm gonna protect my bar."

There was a rustle of noise, and a few women in v-cut dresses screeched and ran from the VIP after seeing Nadia and Hylo with their guns drawn. A man emerged from the back, he was shivering and white-suited and confused.

"What the fuck is going on here?" he said. He held his hands up. Nadia immediately recognized him. She started to move away from Hylo to shoot Dr. Cobbler in his bulgy temple. Hylo kept one eye on her and cocked his gun, and she prepared to take him out him, too, but he swung his arm around and shot a bullet through Dr. Cobbler's head.

He threw the gun on the floor, kicked it to her, and raised his hands in surrender. Nadia fell back, stunned. Her gun was still drawn, and fury and relief and chilly fear washed her clean. She looked back at Hylo and, with her free hand carefully picked up his gun too and pointed both at him. Still. Still. Still.

"You stole that from me. That was big," she spit, keeping her voice a steady line.

"I told you you're not a criminal," he said, then softly, "Nadia."

"You don't know me," she said but lowered her gun. She didn't know why she lowered it.

Because he did know her, didn't he? She didn't know how, but he somehow knew her. He walked toward her slowly, as if she were a bomb ready to detonate, as if he were gauging her reaction. He gestured toward her gloved hand.

"I know what's under the glove. TH1-MONICA. That's your real name. I gave you that name when I was working on you with Dr. Cobbler. Now you're Nadia."

His name in her mouth sounded like violet petals swinging.

He kept coming forward. "You loved me. A real long time ago. You lost your memories in the War, but I knew I'd find you in some iteration of time. It took me a while, waiting for you, getting this job, figuring out when you'd arrive, but I knew you'd come to this one. If not for me, for revenge."

He reached out a hand, and she took a step back.

"I'm my own daughter," she said, but her voice sounded soft. She looked at his face and remembered the scent of his smile. Cigarettes and cherry blossoms. Why? When had she been so close? What about love? Wasn't it just fine to love? Couldn't she be her own woman and still love?

"Of course you are," he said. "But come on. Remember me, too."

He reached over, softly swept a loc from her face, and pressed the side of her temple sharply.

She remembered him too, then. The lithe dark-browed soldier-scientist who watched Dr. Cobbler make hybrids of tech and humans at MIT. Dr. Cobbler was the originator of her kind of Tech in the first place. Hylo had once believed Tech and humans and hybrids could co-exist. Still he was always attached to Dr. Cobbler, his professor, a mirror of him, the one who had created Nadia and the other Tech. Hylo risked everything to leave Dr. Cobbler after the doctor sold his Tech to the American government, and Hylo was always on the run. But Hylo wasn't like Dr. Cobbler, was he? He was fair and kind-minded, not angry. Still, his pseudo-father tried to destroy hybrids and humans and tech altogether by reprogramming all of the tech he'd created to kill humans. Humans, of course, saw Tech as the enemy, and they fought back, resulting in the War. Hybrids were also on the chopping block even though they were both human and Tech. Dr. Cobbler, apparently, simply wanted to Watch the World Blaze before he burned it all down, as men like him always did. And so he burned it.

Her family went first, killed by humans who hated both tech and hybrids. And she escaped, helped by a woman called Northern who guided her across sleek rivers, following moonlight, where she had no thirst nor slake.

Mr. Cobbler's reprogramming hadn't worked on her, and she never knew why. After many years of running on her own, she met up with Hylo in a short bar on Broadway in Nashville. He was a bartender there too. She didn't remember him back then either. They kept finding themselves, again and again, in different cities. Back then, he'd erased her memories, too, and without them, she went running.

The hard part was when Hylo and Nadia fell in love. A secret kiss under a sloped, fresh-bloomed Sakura tree. She was sitting on the bench, reading, and he came over and said roughly, "When you're done reading, get up and kiss me." So she finished a few pages, then got up and kissed him. Then, there was a cuddle on a Massachusetts baycliff. She'd catch helicopter seeds in her hands and watch them fall, and he said something about how the cloven things were always spinning, like her. There were hard times, too. When he'd saved her from exploding houses and cherry bombs from the humans, other times she'd saved him from human snipers and Tech rifles. She showed him how to ride a motorcycle and he bought his own, red, and drove it down Hillwood. All of these moments of high and low drama amounted to love, and of course, when Mr. Cobbler found out about the two, he went after her in Nashville, too.

Hylo helped her escape back then, and she watched him disappear in a swift explosion of the bar meant for both of them, never to return. She was saved by Maya Dream, the graduate assistant, who had created a time portal a long while back. She also had erased Nadia's memories of Hylo, given her the mission simply to Kill Dr. Cobbler, Save Us All so the robot-girl went back in time to stop the destruction. She remembered Maya and Dr. Cobbler, but never Hylo nor the supposed death of him. She knew she had a family who she must avenge, but she could never remember their faces.

Yet. She had forgotten about what had happened in the past. It was old and worn and gone. Why hadn't she remembered? Hylo was still here.

It wasn't just because he and Maya had reprogrammed her to forget about horror or trauma or the human family who raised her. They wanted her to live purely. She had forgotten everything, but still, she hadn't forgotten the traumatic parts. All she knew was that she needed Dr. Cobbler to die. Why had she forgotten all of Hylo's love? Why had he reprogrammed her to forget both the good and the horrible? She wanted to at least have That Good even if she had the horrible, too.

Here he was before her. Grizzled as much as he could be with scattered scruff, his skin was always brown and sweet and soft. Here he was alive. Her eyes wet quickly, and he shook his head.

"You're not a crier in this iteration of time. I noticed that immediately. You used to cry all the time back when I met you. You're a robot but such a fucking feeler," he laughed. She opened her mouth to say something else but the Men without Guns had returned.

They were red-faced, eyes smoking. One of them lunged after Hylo, and he wrestled him down. She used the Big Guy's momentum against him to flip the other guy down, and she gave him a solitary kick in the balls too.

"Let's get the fuck out of here," he said. "Ven conmigo si tú quieres…"

She punched a guy away from Hylo, and he yanked her away from an incoming kick from another bouncer. Barely getting away, they bounded down the stairs and fell out of the bar.

"So what do we do now that we're trapped here in the past?" she said.

He grabbed his keys jangled them. "My apartment's open tonight. You can meet me there. I'm going to have to go deal with this shit inside. Looks like we fixed the future though."

"You still have that old motorcycle? The Wild One?"

"Of course. Parked out back." He tossed her the keys, and she caught them.

Outside, she approached the corner of the sidewalk and saw it immediately. Purpl'd like her locs. He'd painted it from his signature scarlet. The huge, lighted city air cut against her skin, and she usually couldn't feel human things like wind, but today, she felt it, a breath of sharp ice as cold as her hand. She got on the bike, ripped off her glove, exposing hard wire and silver. She started the engine, felt the wild rush of the bike, the steel-cold night, and the possibility of snow. She flew off, into the glorious black city, alone or perhaps not.

Woman with a Scarf by Eliezer Miranda

Sapphics in Softball (Isn't That the Same Word?)

by Salem B. Holden

I think when we met
our souls said
"Hi,

I remember you—
the little dyke boy on third
(or did you play short stop,
first base,
and catcher
when they needed you
too?)"—We
never really talked about
what position we liked

Just more talked about
playing the game.

Ode to Poetry

by Salem B. Holden

I was thinking about you
when I saw the royal blue billboard
"The clear choice!" healthcare workers smiling
and a car came up and smashed
my mercury magick soul stitch heart
into four chambers with one last final part

The healthcare workers ran out of the sign
Defibrillator and sonnet stencil attached
"Their iambic pentameter is off by two beats,
get the no. 2 sharpened Narcan stat!
We need an internal rhyme or innuendo (or
maybe an allusion thrown in here somewhere
nowhere down anywhere, where is where anyhow?)"

Two rhyme schemes later my eyes
unglued and a cosmic shift later
a gray feather quill medaled melded
to my hand
the healthcare workers ran back
into the billboard thumbs up whispering
"The clear choice."

Untitled by Cottonbro

three queers in a Subaru go to a basement show

by Liam Strong

it's supposed to sound / like a joke cuz it is / "Abandon lying" / said the bill
/ -board / we stole two potatoes / from the Citgo / just outside Clare MI /
anemone of sprout / grayed coral / i tucked one / under the driver's / seat Simon
/ so its eyes can't / ogle you / tits freshly dissected / & gone / i've once eaten a
baked / potato this way / you just remove / the excess / & they won't bother / you
Brian / but it's fine / i'm not expecting / you to indulge / though we can't afford /
a Red / Roof Inn / the joke is that / there's no proverb / of straight here / maybe
the knob / of roots tough / as concrete can / hide for us / so we can / be out in the
open / i know / right / it wasn't even worth / laughing to my / -self

literature review of simpler times

by Liam Strong

classic story of girl meets boy meets non-boy meets world. classic complications, tensions, sex scenes. classic story of neutral earth. classic vibes in classic towns with classic neon. classic story about pre-transition child stealing cigarettes for his mother from Admiral Tobacco. he's classically cute, he's funny, he's dying. classic fable about two metaphors being the same emotional height. classic story of the monster devouring its sibling, then an entire village. classic story of sherpa-lined attitude, opposite sexes with ample similarity. classic story of the gender-bending liquid metal Terminator who disintegrates in a bath of molten steel. classic story of faggots burning on Turner Classic Movies. classic story of giving no context & receiving zero commentary. Ramones in Russia somewhere beyond the background, cake on the lower lip, Alicia Silverstone in Clueless but also not—all classic narrative details. classic husband thievery story, classic synonyms for facade in every story. a distant father in the apartment complex next door yearns for when kids liked classic stories, required reading in school. classic stories—like death having very little to do with death. classic stories such as Macbeth, Freddie Mercury, The Fault in our Stars, Macbeth. classically iconic, the protagonist functions as their own antagonist. classic stories don't involve so much politics. classic stories on pre-existing conditions & not so much speculation, deliberation. in classic stories, the reader is not supposed to see themselves in the mirror of the page. in classic stories, queerness is easily defined. in classic stories, the dead stay dead as long as need be.

BREAKING: one man dead from Bikini Kill crowd, no one cares

by Liam Strong

---

the lip of the Sprite can is a blade. it's tenable that the definition of a blade is a thin concept, broad & elastic over my binding. belief like skim milk, zero percent, belief in what's there, my pussy or dick or whatever you want to name them. hypothesis of underwear, abstract of the underworld. my tits, my anti-tits, my tongue which looks like any other. if i remove both ankles, then i have no weakness. Achilles is the lesser of two lessons—one that he is worth discussing at all. the other that his name means we will suffer from sorrow in his wake. a man on the edge of the pit keeps trying to get my attention between songs & i want to smell petrichor in the aluminum. it's like wanting the reek of blood even though skin harbors its release. it's unfair. when i need to be split wide open & have my tendons rearranged, bloody steel just won't cut it. no, i don't want to be fucked, i don't want to be made love to, i don't want to have sex or any of its other pseudonyms & etymologies, no. crowds around me make existing look so simple, my body & its other bodies on a day-to-day basis, like apples & bananas oxidizing into conclusion. research shows decay depends on the organism, which explains a lot. so much. that i'm here, always living & dying my best life, shoving unnecessary flesh into places it doesn't belong.

The Reformation of a Tomboy

by Hannah Birss

When my breasts began to bud
and my body began to bleed,
I threw my femininity out
in the trash with my tampons
for the fear of being less.

I didn't want to be like other girls -
vapid, silly, tittitering objects
of both lust and dismissal.
I wanted to be seen.
So I burped with the boys,
swallowed worms on dares,
and came home bloodied
with proud black eyes.

I watched the girls
with jealousy and admiration,
shoved myself in the closet
like an old baggy sweater.
I dressed myself down
in dowdy, shapeless clothes.
Fear became the root
and insecurity the tree.

It took twenty years to realize
That I am not confined to the binary
that others might impose;
validation is nothing
in the face of self-actualization.

Now, I play dress-up everyday,
With a tickle trunk arsenal

Of perfumes, makeup, and shoes.
I am sweet and sexual,
draped curves like candy
and painted nails like claws.
I kiss the girls, and dress like one.
I make the boys stare,
And then kiss them too.
If either look down their noses
Or think me less
for my opulent decorations
or joyful promiscuity, their loss -
I'll blow a kiss to my mirror
And be on my way.
My god, I'm hot.

Lunar Orgasms

by Venus Fultz

Plum wine for Xem

Weed honey for me

Every curvature of movement

Tinga-linga-lings my

Boi pussy. Who needs

Words when you're fucking

The moon.

Eating the Rich

by Lauren Tivey

Lemmy's raspy main vocal
reverberating in stereo, and
back then our speakers were
the size of compact foreign
cars. Legend has it he slept
with over 1,000 women,
despite a rather unfortunate
prominent mole, a signature
feature earning him ugly status.
Some metalhead did the math:
50 years ÷ 20 women per year
= 2.5 women per month. He bawls
to Motörhead's thrashing beat,
and I understand that if I ever
had the chance, yes, I would.
Those mutton chops, accent,
the hat, tight jeans, leather
boots. That straining voice.
Something about a sexy-ugly
man, a grotesque attraction.
The fleshy mole beckons;
how my teeth would gnash
and rip, blood spurting on
the pillow. We'd laugh and
patch it up, make breakfast
in the morning before he
kicked me out, because
that's rock 'n roll, baby.
You eat it while you can.

Devil Dolls

by Lauren Tivey

Black suede thigh-high boots
 embroidered up to there

chunky heels, roses and vines
    fishnets, push-up bra

fire engine red velvet dress
 maybe figurative—and pointed

claws to match, horns literal—
    tail, too. How we strutted in

like dangerous Hollywood starlets
 the makeshift pitchfork prop

past security, but still they confiscated
    at the door; Alice Cooper concert

Hampton Beach Casino Ballroom
 me, blonde demon

just before Halloween, early aughts
    with my #1 girlfriend

tempestuous redheaded Judi
 already smudged

a psycho cat, her painted whiskers
    with too much whiskey

from too much fun, and Alice onstage
 the packed sweaty bodies

in his top hat, maestro of ceremonies
    all Hell's children pressing

together under an orgiastic disco ball
	weed cloud wafting

blowing out our fragile eardrums
	and all the shaggy wolf boys

shook our sweet asses to the music
	having the best night

throwing out psychedelic prisms
	the speakers of doom

voices hoarse from squealing, and we
	were salivating, and we blew kisses

two laughing, luscious, lip-stained vamps
	in our young, damned lives.

Woman by Mohammad Metri

Almost Sixty-Barbie Plans for Retirement

by Anjanette Delgado

Barbie nearing sixty
is sexy,
slender, too thin,
really, reads by the pool
magazines;
never newspapers,
which damage her
glittery AF manicure,
the better to blind
lifeguards whose names
were never really Ken.

She takes a selfie
with Skipper, her bestie
who's really her daughter
from that time when confused,
she let GI Joe feel
above the hem of her
high-waisted baby doll dress,
saying, Oh hell,
what's a girl made of material to do?

She knows one day
they'll want to convict her
for her complacency
in the murder of millions
of girls, and hopes
to be long gone by then,
camper and all,
in a still-fifty-something flash,
no time to sling a smile

for the paparazzi.

And yet, her plan won't work,
she knows she was never
the smartest doll in the box, those
press bastards will catch her
in a doll-breaking minute,
no all-American lifeguard
to help her swim to Sweden,
where she's never been to
and cannot begin to know
how to get to.

Feline Woman by Kizko Pop

Miss Pink by Pawel Szvmanski

Girl, Uninterrupted:
On Christina Aguilera, *Stripped,* and Growing Up with the Raunch Culture of the 2000s

by Alyssa Favreau

Stripped begins with a twenty-two-year-old Christina Aguilera reintroducing herself to her listeners. For all the cacophony of Y2K synthesizers and overlaid newscasters speculating on yet another scandal – part distorted descent into another dimension, part surround sound cinematic opening – the album's first track is surprisingly subdued. With very little fanfare the singer informs us that she will be speaking her mind and showing us how she really feels. There will be no hype, no pretense. Just Christina, stripped.

The year is 2003 and the singer's fourth album practically lives in the little blue boombox perched beside my bed, guzzling eight D batteries every time I inevitably forget to plug it in. I'm thirteen; I've just started high school. Without the buffer of a junior high, I've left the safe confines of a sheltered elementary school for the lawlessness of the local "party" high school. I sit and listen to the music on a pink and green comforter under a recently tacked up Orlando Bloom poster and my killer whale light switch plate, reeling from the culture shock and my own roiling hormones.

Stripped is in many ways the best musical example of a star's dramatic public break from her child persona. For all that my white, middle-class childhood lacks in resemblance to the realities described in the album, it is my guide through the transition from kid to teen. I have experienced neither the romantic manipulations of "Walk Away" nor the domestic violence of "I'm OK," instead my main hardship is a truly dizzying array of unrequited crushes, yet

Christina's music is what best reflects the overwhelm I feel at this age. *Stripped* is an outlier as I shed the Canadian pop punk of Avril Lavigne and Sum41 for a Cool Girl blend of grunge and seventies rock, but it is the perfect balm to soothe the mundane cruelties of early adolescence. It's the music I turn to, and return to, as I navigate the eighth grade.

—

High school is exciting; there's no denying that. Part of me is exhilarated by these new freedoms: my own locker, a class schedule that I'm responsible for maintaining, the solo bus ride home. It's also a time captured in the diary I keep from the ages of eleven to fourteen. Modeled after Meg Cabot's *Princess Diaries* series, the diary spans two ratty notebooks and is filled with direct address entries in blue ballpoint pen that describe events as they happen, with timestamps separating moments stolen during classes and between chores. The result is an intriguing primary document, an artifact left by someone I no longer fully recognize but who keenly needs to make sense of her world.

In one entry, I recount my attendance at the first dance of the year: "At 1st I felt really out of place 'cuz I like can't dance at all, but then I let loose. And when I say let loose, I *mean* let loose. I mean ass-shaking, etc ..." My first impressions vary: grinding is "not that gross," the strobe lights provided by a local radio station are "really annoying," the event's two-hour duration is insufficient, "cuz for some ppl (me) it takes almost an hour for the ice to break." Nevertheless, I dance with four boys, with at least one awkward encounter undoubtedly soundtracked by Christina herself, and consider the evening a triumph.

The five-time platinum *Stripped* is also wildly successful. There are, of course, the expected hysterical reviews: *Entertainment* deems Christina "desperate and shrill," *Brandweek* worries about her "self-imposed exile [to] Skankville," and *Time* finds her look perfect for an "intergalactic hooker convention" (a description that begs several questions, namely "What planet hosts this convention?" and "Can I go?"). But the five singles that appear on the Billboard Hot 100 and the album's five Grammy nominations handily drown out any negativity.

Via *Billboard*, Christina declares that she and her new "Xtina" persona are just "being a little brash and having fun with it," explaining that by grabbing attention first with "Dirrty" and then "hit[ting] them with the one-two punch of 'Beautiful' next, and 'Fighter,' … you realize it's all done with a purpose." Christina is clear in her album promotion that she's "showcasing the many sides of being a strong woman: a little bit of owning your sexuality, being able to be vulnerable and owning your vulnerability, and then being able to stand up for yourself and own your past."

It's a multifaceted approach that's undeniably effective, and for a young girl looking for confidence and validation, the album is fertile ground. From the well-known singles "Can't Hold Us Down," "Fighter," and "Beautiful," to deeper cuts like "Soar," "The Voice Within," and "Keep On Singing My Song," self-empowerment is an endlessly malleable theme, and one of which I am in desperate need. Indeed, by September 29, I am already well and truly disillusioned with my surroundings:

> You know, I hate society, I really do. I hate how women are objectified [*sic*] but they still do it because they like the attention. I hate how guys think they're so cool when they have like, 3 girls, and, I'm not saying it's right to do that, but if a girl does it, she's labelled a whore. I hate how if you don't wear really revieling [*sic*] clothing, guys don't notice you.

It's a proto-feminist ethos cribbed straight from the album, the hip hop and R&B Lil' Kim joint "Can't Hold Us Down" in particular. Christina belting out a manifesto about gendered double standards and slut shaming has clearly made an impact but, while her conclusion is celebratory, my outlook is markedly less rosy. "The worst part is, I can't change any of it, because there's only one of me, and a whole batallion [*sic*] of people who like it the way it is," I exclaim. Then, as if soliloquizing the height of my dramatic adolescent melancholia, I add: "Ah life! Why must thy be littered w/ frustration & disapointment [*sic*]." We can blame a

Shakespeare-forward Enriched English class for this last affectation.

In *The Second Sex*, Simone de Beauvoir describes the pubescent girl as someone who "feels that her body is getting away from her." She writes, "it is no longer the straightforward expression of her individuality; [the body] becomes foreign to her; and at the same time she becomes for others a thing: on the street men follow her with their eyes and comment on her anatomy. She would like to be invisible; it frightens her to become flesh." I had by this point already become such an object, such flesh, my existence dotted with construction crews stopping their work as I passed, bus drivers leeringly telling me I didn't have to pay the fare – events so confusing to a child they don't appear in my diary even as they're forever etched in my memory.

By 2003, I hardly need the lessons of "Soar," in which powerfully uplifting piano chords give way to a much more somber bridge. Christina's soft falsetto channels de Beauvoir while telling of a girl who comes face to face with her fears in the mirror, her reflection unrecognizable after years of trying to become someone else. By this point, the world is already reflecting someone different back at me, more grown, more trapped, and unlike Christina, I don't have a gospel choir arriving for a last verse and triumphant finish. The world I've entered into is much more explicitly sexual than the one I've so recently left, and I find myself wholly unequipped for it. I'm not at risk of losing my sense of self, but rather bewildered to see that self reflected back in ways I do not recognize and do not want.

"I didn't tell u about the thong incident," I write on October 8, "[w]e were in drama and Scott told me I should wear a thong. Yes he did, I'm not kidding." It's an order couched in all the reckless ownership thirteen-year-old boys feel for the bodies of thirteen-year-old girls. I respond with "Y should I make myself suffer by wearing a kind of underwear no ones going to c anyway?" Scott's retort, "you have to suffer to be sexy," is met with an eye roll in the moment and a "what nerve!" in the diary, yet I'm left deeply conflicted.

I'm growing up in what psychologist Mary Pipher, in *Reviving Ophelia: Saving the Selves of Adolescent Girls*, terms a "girl-poisoning culture." The 1994 book was read and annotated by my mother as I was coming into my teenage years. *Reviving Ophelia* charts an increasingly sexualized and media-saturated culture and its effects on pubescent girls, whose wholeness is at risk of being "shattered by the chaos of adolescence." For Pipher, it is especially "bright and sensitive girls [who] are most at risk" of this splintering, who are most likely "to understand the implications of the media around them and be alarmed." (Thanks for highlighting this passage, Mom.) Pipher continues:

> They have the mental equipment to pick up our cultural ambivalence about women, and yet they don't have the cognitive, emotional and social skills to handle this information ... They struggle to resolve the unresolvable and to make sense of the absurd.

As I enter high school, I am – to paraphrase a different popstar – not a girl, and not yet interested in being a woman. At least not like I see them in the world.

A *Rolling Stone* review that comes out in late 2002 calls *Stripped* "almost an album for grown-ups," and months later I continue to inhabit a similar space. At 6:25 p.m. on September 21, 2003, I revel in the fact that "Mom says she doesn't like my new eyeliner on me." I'm incapable, however, of fully embodying the rebellious teen. Although her disapproval bodes well, I still cling to a childish relationship with my parents, one that is as present and obliging as it is trying to be combative and disengaged. I might be glad that my mother says the eyeliner "makes my eyes too dark," but in the same breath I nevertheless "G2G make hors-d'oevres [*sic*]" for a dinner we're about to host, a chipper little helper in aspirationally dangerous makeup.

In this space after childhood but before adolescence, I am caught in a terrifying no man's land between warring impulses. Wanting to be desired by my peers but terrified of what that desire might imply, my behavior can't always be justified. About an hour before disclosing the thong incident, I write that:

> [J]ust so you know, I'm not talking to Jin Soo [on MSN Messenger]
> anymore cuz last time I did we were having a very enjoyable conversation
> until right b4 he left, he asked if I would 'do it' w/ him if I was old
> enough! Sorry, but I will not keep talking to a guy who just asked me if I
> would want to have sex w/ him! So I blocked & deleted him.

It's a reaction that puzzles me now. I had a crush on this boy, who had posited a fairly harmless and unlikely hypothetical scenario. Surely some sort of reprimand would have been enough to end the conversation. But thirteen-year-old me finds this sort of gaze terrifying – "I know guys get horny and stuff, but still! I mean, it's never been about me. *shiver*" – and lashes out.

I'm not the only one feeling at once desiring of, yet threatened by, this new sort of attention. That same day I recount how "Amin supposedly has a crush on Paige and supposedly once you get to know him, he's really creepy and stalkerish. Anyway, she wants him to go away, so next time he talks to me, I'm supposed to tell him that Paige wants him to 'Fuck off.'" My friend was experiencing unwanted attention, clearly, but one with a doubled edge: "Also, this other guy, Thomas, asked her out. She said no (of course), but now she can't groan about no one liking her! She's really starting the year off well, isn't she? Unlike some ppl (me)." The irony is not lost on me that I whip from support for Paige to being jealous of the romantic interest paid to her, all while seemingly unable to connect my MSN escapades to her situation. Half a century earlier, de Beauvoir calls this a "diffuse hopefulness," a desire that lives in "ideal mists" rather than in the "hand, mouth, and flesh" of another real person. In the moment, however, it feels more hopeless than anything else.

"This is the trait that characterizes the young girl and gives us the key to most of her behavior," writes de Beauvoir, who continues: "She does not accept the destiny assigned to her by nature and by society, and yet she does not repudiate it completely; she is too much divided against herself to join battle with the world." It's a perfect description for the version of me who instinctively does not want to become a sexual object but wants boys to like her, who wants to shock her parents but will help them arrange appetizers prettily on a plate. "Each of her desires has its corresponding anxiety," says de Beauvoir, explaining the paradox of this age: "She is eager to come into possession of her future, but she dreads to break with her past; she wants to 'have' a man, but she does not want him to have her as his prey." I'll learn a darker truth years later. The underlying story of that first dance where I feel so uninhibited is that a group of grade twelve boys have made a bet to see who can have sex with a grade eight girl. I may not be consciously aware of this predatory gaze while enjoying my newfound "ass-shaking" capabilities, but at least some part of me can sense the underlying threat that permeates much of my world.

—

At thirteen, I need the complexities of *Stripped*. If the album had been only the beguiling Latin pop of "Infatuation" or the beguiled neo-soul of "Loving Me 4 Me" it wouldn't have been able to contain the full scope of my feelings. Neither would the heartening gospel of "Keep on Singing My Song," nor the equally righteous anger of the flamenco-rock track "Makeover," have been able to single-handedly hold my interest. At thirteen, I need to be seduced by "Walk Away," gassed up by "Underappreciated," and held by "The Voice Within." At thirteen, I need to be hardened by "Fighter," to know that every slight – real or perceived – has the potential to make me that much stronger, harder, and wiser.

"Fighter" is a testament to how unfair the world can be, from the single's first line that Christina all but growls out to the guitar-heavy crescendo that punctuates the "you, can't, stop, me" of the bridge before splintering into echoing voices that come together only to vow that they've had enough. The music video, too, showcases a uniquely feminine ability to recover and rebuild after adversity, with director Floria Sigismondi's signature desaturated goth style that borrows liberally from post-grunge aesthetics. In a loose interpretation of the moth's lifecycle, every step Christina takes in the video, from escaping a glass cocoon to removing insect pins from her back, brings her closer to her final form. She then emerges as a silky, ethereal creature somewhere between pupa and adult moth, and in full possession of the knowledge that she is capable of pulling through.

If "Fighter" shows me anything, it is that there can be strength where there is fragility; it's something songwriting titan Linda Perry, responsible for several of *Stripped*'s tracks, puts to use throughout the album. "I know it sounds ghoulish," Perry will later divulge when discussing the deeply personal "I'm OK," "and she didn't think she could do it, but I made her do the song in tears." A chronicle of Christina's father's physical abuse of her mother, "I'm OK" is a moment of gut-wrenching vulnerability. The singer's vocal grain is raw and wounded as she sings, unable to stand, from the recording studio floor; it is Perry in particular who fights for this lack of polish and painful emotionality to remain in the songs' final versions.

Even the spoken instruction to look away that opens "Beautiful" is a candid moment and a glimpse at Christina's shyness: she tells the friend who has accompanied her into the recording booth for support that she can't bear to be observed. Much ink has been spilled on the Grammy Song of the Year–nominated "Beautiful," on its beauty and on the importance of a song so unreserved in its love for its listeners, and it's the first sung line in particular that I always return to. The immediate heel turn from Christina's day being wonderful to the singer finding it hard to breathe rings so true for me in this period of constant hormonal change. In one moment, I am incapable of finding a redeeming quality in myself, and in the next I am my own staunchest defender.

"I am the most stupid, pathetic, thick, dum [*sic*], crappy, imbecilic, idiotic, not intelligent, crazy, insane, stupid, stupid, stupid excuse for a teenage girl," I write in early October. I have just told a boy that I like him, and it has not gone well. In this moment, I can only reproach myself for the ill-advised admission. Two hours later, however, I've mulled over the situation and decided that his reaction, of looking me up and down before uttering a single, devastating "ew," is unacceptable. I am incensed: "And the ironic thing is, I still like him. Yup, that's right, I still like the complete imbecile that told Magda I was 'too smart for him.' Ha! Damn right, I am!"

"Girls become fragmented," writes Pipher, "[t]hey are confident in the morning and overwhelmed with anxiety by nightfall." Christina, at least, can keep up with my wild incongruities, seems to understand the need to feel sexy, despairing, thrilled, furious, sometimes all in the same hour, sometimes all in the same album. Not fragmented, then, but refracting every possibility.

—

My well-thumbed copy of *Cosmogirl!* magazine's March 2003 issue serves as a template for how I'll come to think about *Stripped*-era Christina, that month's cover model. The article features a large close-up of the singer's bared back – her contrapposto stance adorned with only a backless sequined shrug, geometric gold earrings, and boldly scripted Xtina tattoo. Across from the photo, the magazine pronounces that they "have a strong suspicion that the new look, the clothes (or lack of!) are all a part of an ingenious plan – a mask, her way of protecting her inner self from an industry that thrives on gossip and ridicule." It's a fundamentally sympathetic profile, one that acknowledges a certain overexposure but frames it as preventative oversharing designed to create distance between the public persona and the real person beneath it. "It's as if she's thinking, Here! Here's something to talk about," the profile declares, doing some of Christina's image-building for her before continuing, "[w]hile you're ripping me to shreds on these surface things, I'll be over here figuring out who I am, like every other 22-year-old." In this interpretation, the new persona is just smokescreen, a distraction from the real person busy finding out who they are.

Cosmogirl!'s position is one that is unexpectedly understanding, but one unfortunately overwhelmed by the cognitive whiplash of the 2000s – as demonstrated in miniature by the teen magazine's coverlines. The issue's main promise to let its readers "Find Out Who [Christina] Really Is" is easily drowned out by other, bolder coverlines. "Get Flatter Abs In Two Weeks!" and "be a great kisser (here's how)" vacillate between promise and command; "ARE YOU SEXY? see page 42" dispenses with any pretense altogether. The profile's second accompanying photograph features Christina pulling back her black-and-blonde hair (with its mess of half-hearted braids) to reveal the beginnings of a confident snarl. The rest of the image, however, is a full-body shot complete with tall boots, minuscule shorts, and a large swath of lower abdomen that fits right in with the rest of the issue's exhortations to achieve the "perfect look."

In 2005's *Female Chauvinist Pigs,* Ariel Levy acts as cultural anthropologist for the newly risen phenomenon she calls "raunch culture," a *Playboy* revival–meets–*Girls Gone Wild* moment with which I'm all too familiar. For Levy, raunch culture "isn't about opening our minds to the possibilities and mysteries of sexuality. It's about endlessly reiterating one particular – and particularly commercial – shorthand for sexiness."

According to Levy, raunch culture combines backlash against the perceived prudishness of second-wave feminism with the rise of salacious reality television and increased access to internet pornography. The hyper-sexualized and hyper-gendered phenomenon then provides the perfect opportunity to promote – and commercialize – one homogenous way of being, a culture that Levy believes does a particular disservice to teenagers:

> By any measure, the way we educate young people about sexuality is
> not working. We expect them to dismiss their instinctive desires and
> curiosities even as we bombard them with images that imply that lust
> is the most important appetite and hotness the most impressive virtue.
> Somehow, we expect people who are by definition immature to make
> sense of this contradictory mishmash.

As I attempt to become a sexual being at the height of raunch culture's power, I certainly cannot find my way out of the contradiction. I do, however, feel a growing need to explore romantic and sexual desire. The song "Get Mine, Get

Yours," for example, strikes me as thrillingly risqué – something that likely says more about my young age than anything else. Christina wanting to have her sex life resemble a nine to five job is so lacking in eroticism that it could only ever have appealed to a thirteen-year-old ignorant of both sex and full-time employment.

I want to submerge myself in the album's more pleasurable moments, to share in Christina's first loves and deep connections. But something prevents me from fully embracing the contagious certainty with which she preaches her Shout Out Loud philosophy in songs like "Can't Hold Us Down." I can't help but notice that in the music video Christina herself wears the same sort of small velour outfit that sets my teeth on edge when donned by my classmates. How loud can a message of rebellious desire ring when it comes from a place of adherence?

The music video for "Dirrty" is the flashpoint for this conflict. The song is in many ways a reclamation of power. Christina has paid her dues and she's in the mood for some fun. A sequel of sorts to Redman's "Let's Get Dirty (I Can't Get in Da Club)," Christina can, and does, revel in a night of hedonism and reckless abandon. I will always have a soft spot for "Dirrty." Everything works for me, from the beat that samples multiple elements of Redman's original, to the rapper's none-too-serious guest verse, to Christina's own barn-burning riff that goes on for a full eight count. But there's a slipperiness to the visual elements – one that doesn't come from the video's liberal use of water, sweat, mud, and engine oil – that leaves me ill at ease.

As iconic as the visuals have become – no one will ever see a bikini paired with chaps and not make the association – they play into a voyeurism that doesn't fully challenge preconceived beliefs about young women's sexualities. Look beyond the bodybuilders, furries, and contortionists and what's left is costuming and choreography that feature little, plaid schoolgirl skirts and suggestive glimpses of bright red underwear. Worse is the boxing ring set and the inclusion of posters promoting the sex tourism industry in Thailand. One poster reads "Young Underage Girls," something director David LaChapelle says was an oversight but is nevertheless indicative of the thoughtlessness with which these gritty ingredients are combined to achieve that perfect 2000s raunch.

Despite Christina's lyrics about wanting to get dirrty and get hers, she can't teach me how to authentically connect with my own sexuality. The inherent performativity of popstardom hews too closely to raunch culture's prioritization of desirability over desire. I know what I must do to be wanted, no matter how much it might chafe. What I don't know how to do, or rather, what I'm not given permission to do, is want. I can be looked at, not look. I can be acted upon, even set the stage for the acting, but never act myself. However positive the messages in the album's singles might be, they remain constantly undermined by the corresponding visuals. I am told that the world's double standards regarding women are cruel ("Can't Hold Us Down"), that I must fight for myself ("Fighter") because I am worthy just as I am ("Beautiful") and deserve to have fun ("Dirrty"), but also that it's necessary to do it all while never deviating from the standards of hotness of the day. Christina may have her detractors, but Xtina is in many ways raunch culture's ideal.

By virtue of existing within the music industry, Christina needs to be wanted, needs to court that wanting. Everything else is in service to that external desire. Everything else comes second. Though the media narrative depicts the singer in perfect control of her career, artistry, and sexual image, which empower her and give her pleasure, the fact remains that her decisions are incredibly financially lucrative. A cynical perspective would see the release of "Beautiful," hot on the heels of "Dirrty," as image management, a way to mitigate the criticism levied against the hyper-sexual first single. So, how much of the bold and hyper-sexed aesthetic is an authentic desire to shake off an outgrown and undesired little-girl image; how much is a calculated move to differentiate a corporate brand in a Britney-saturated market; and, when it comes to the business of pop music, does the distinction really matter?

A couple decades later and I'm now living in a post-*Barbie* world where frothy feminist empowerment can be found only as long as you ignore the corporate money-making foundations it rests on. There is no way to fully escape consumption – capitalistic or otherwise. But how much freer, not to mention queerer, would my teenage years have been had I not been busy struggling against the rigidity of the sexuality I saw laid out before me? If I hadn't been so concerned with repudiating what was offered and had had the opportunity to pursue what I newly wanted instead?

Regardless, on November 29, 2003, at 1:36pm, I find myself hating "all the stupid ppl that judge me b4 they know me. I hate the way I don't fit [in]. Normally, this wouldn't bother me, except, deep down, I sorta want to fit in." Throughout the diary, I fluctuate between conformity and rebellion, trying and often failing to find the authenticity that exists between the two.

Then and now, I live in these in-between spaces, and I now find that I have no interest in denying Christina the same halting, not-always-successful attempts at navigating between acceptance and unruliness. Perhaps, I too am guilty of projecting too simplistic an image onto a woman just coming into her own. In one of the album's quieter interludes, Christina apologizes for not being either a virgin or a slut, telling us that no matter how much we dismantle her into easily digestible parts, she will remain whole and complicated. Maybe there, too, she's speaking to me.

—

Stripped caught me at a curious moment as I moved from boy band to dad rock. I doubt the album would have made the same impact had it come out two years in either direction. It would be the last time I felt connected to Christina, who waited four years before releasing her next album. The jazz and soul–inspired collection, with its mid-century pinup aesthetic and odes to a new husband, resonated less with a teenager in the late 2000s, and by that point my tastes had veered more toward a Franz Ferdinand–flavored indie rock. Christina went *Back to Basics*, and I lost interest.

The singer now looks back on the *Stripped*-era as a "rough patch," telling *Rolling Stone* that "I was going through a lot of personal stuff. Even my hair color going dark. I was in a dark place." It almost feels like a betrayal of that moment that meant so much to me. That *Stripped* acknowledged the darkness while managing to rise above it was powerful, and as much as I've searched, I haven't found that power in the rest of Christina's artistic output – as much as tracks like "Still Dirrty" try to convince me that some edginess remains.

Even if Christina's more reserved versions on *Stripped* are more immediately comprehensible to me, I do owe Xtina my gratitude for sparking a journey of femme self-discovery that even today I am certainly not finished with. That her message of self-empowerment was at times muddy and ambivalent was, in the end, entirely in keeping with the time and culture she lived in, and I'm increasingly fine with not having all the answers. Looking back at Christina and at my teenage self, I have fond feelings for two people who were willing to keep growing.

Strangely, Christina's best goodbye comes in the middle of the album. In "Cruz" she is driving away in her car, heat rising as her hand floats languidly through the air. She sings of an inner child who will always be sitting beside her in calm companionship. Christina knows she must leave the past behind, not to escape but to flourish in ways that are as yet unknown. Thirteen-year-old me didn't know exactly what she wanted either, but she knew there must be more out there. Two decades later and I'm still on the same beautiful ride, still searching – and that child is surprisingly good company.

Untitled by Allan Franca Carmo

Bankrupt(cy)

by Jen Schneider

Bed Bath & Beyond
filed for bankruptcy

-- again

this past week.

with
this round, it appears the
big box (and its coupon-clipping
fanbase) is either leaving

       leaving   town

or mourning

       a never
       never land

       yellow ducks
       and fairytale sheets

       what's   lost
       what's   found

in and of
an oversized (s)pace,

stuffed of pillows
firm and soft, beds in pristine
form, vacuum cleaners
upright or hand-held,

and cloth

glorious cloth –

satins and cottons,
2000-thread count
pillowcases,
moisturizing face masks,
towels -- extra plush

will be missed.

missed
and treasured –

along with the 99-cent sample
sizes for travel of which we'd
squeeze,
spin, and spiral musk-scented tales
for far-away destinations,

but never venture beyond
our square-mile measure

like those of us born and raised in
neighboring zip codes, who dream
of flight, yet flock instead, tails
between our legs, to well-known
basements and childhood beds

loafers   tucked   cuffed
laces   tied   frayed
beds   unmade   craved
baths   scalding   beyond
wings   chipped   clipped

Aisle 2:

bankrupt. The shame
and stain of dreams

unrealized.

like the 24-hour diner, the one
that cut all hours post-COVID.

a place where morning and
moaning blend. Like a cold brew.

demands for high-end counter
seats and espresso
as much a part of the milieu
as the $9.99 coffee maker.

the store has declared bankruptcy
before. Haven't we all? Only
to find a buyer or
another 20% off coupon
to recharge and renew.

faith (or fate) in a future of
clean sheets, stain-resistant
shower liners,

mildew- and odor-free
everything

the store even had an aisle
with $2.00 confetti. Cans
of Aqua Net brushed
shoulders with Silly String

Aisle 3:

Bed Bath & Beyond
promised new beginnings,
wrinkle-free

but this time
this time appears to be

the end. The end of what,
I think.

I think of the closing sales
the neighbors will surely flock to,
like the blackbirds on the overhead wire

suet comes cheap and the hungry come in droves.
three packs for ten. Six for fifteen. My friends and I
used to collect Bed Bath & Beyond coupons

a golden ticket –
not unlike Willy Wonka and the chocolate bar.

      Sweet.

Aisle 4:

with twenty percent off offerings, we'd stand in line,
count our pennies, and use the discount for pouches,

pouches of Big League Chew

the suburbanites, housewives,
and staged (soon-to-be-empty)
nesters would stare in disbelief

their carts full

      of promise

makeup mirrors and Hollywood lights
kitchen scales and vegetable clippers
electric mixers and OTC elixirs
registry (wedding and baby) checks
back to school bloat (composition
notebooks, hot pots, cascading lights)

      composed

original fairy tales, unoriginal lots
cycles of life, miles of stuff

layaway still a thing
before the days of two-day prime
and expectations in real time

Aisle 5:

delayed gratification
a hallmark
of our childhood. The
Hallmark Channel
our magnificent mile

we'd flip through glossy print
circular smiles of matching sheets,
plush towels, acne cream

we'd stand in line, crack jokes,
and salivate. my cheeks still bear
the crimson shame.

we'd never be one of them

we were less cool than we acted,
but never used coupons
on an automatic fan

we fanned
our coveted coupons with airs
then consumed our Big League Chew

       as if dared

Aisle 6:

it wasn't that we couldn't

afford much else. we couldn't

but didn't care.

We blew our bubbles in carefree form
chewed on little else. Mostly we believed
infinity and beyond was a thing

I wish I had been more generous then
gifted my coupons when I still could

we skimmed coupons
from neighboring mailboxes
and surfed the store's
aisles, happily idle

      welcome   safe

      safe   to be

      anything   and   beyond

      infinity imaginedin real time

a queen in a king-sized bed
a king in a twin-sized sleeper

a 5-star blender
a 4-season rocker
a 3-pronged detangler
a 2-speed recliner

an all-star (Big-League Chew) hitter

an X-Long satin sheet
an X-Small bath towel

      we dreamed

in florals and stripes

in quilted layers and gingham-checked plaid

the store had everything.

Aisle 7:

now Bed Bath & Beyond seeks
to liquidate all stock

the big box era presses, then clogs.
the shame of the toilet plunger and the trash can
the stain of tampons and the condoms

the shame. the stain. too much.
auto-delivery in real-time.

consumption
now monopolized by queries of preferred packaging.
in twelve-point font and deadpan.

Aisle 8:

Bed Bath & Beyond had made it to the big leagues.
unlike many of my Big League Chew chomping crew
can claim. Mostly, we're the same. Those of us still here.
living in a bubble. Once fresh. Now stale.
clipping coupons, accepting of clipped wings

only to return to Earth
from the Nasdaq Exchange

Bed Bath & and Beyond had policies.
policies as reliable as the waterbed buoyancy

returns reliably welcome. double coupons applied.
Aisle 9:

now,

I wonder about bankruptcy's stain

is it possible

to refold quilted corners once undone
and repurpose packages one by one?

when the sum of the parts
strains and stains

what becomes of the coupon
conspiracy shame?

Clean up, in ~~Aisle~~ Chapter 11

That Time Puerto Rico Beat the U.S. By Twenty Points In the First Round of The Olympics

by Jennifer Maritza McCauley

Lebron, Dwayne Wade,
Carmelo Anthony (one of us Afro-Boris)
Alan Iverson,
Tim Duncan
Distracted by
the medium-sized,
thin-boned brown and Black men
hustling and running
and sprinting and shifting
and splitting and dunking and stretching
bunching muscles to win
something of Supposed Meaning,
Something for the Culture.

Dream Team/
Cream Team

This is an easy game to watch, as a family.
Daddy and Tim are for Lebron, my Mami
is for Puerto Rico. Nobody thinks
PR will win.

I am watching them both play, a nerd
who is reading Dick Gregory and Saga comics

until Puerto Rico starts to get ahead.
I'm always for the underdog, in this case
the island against heaving American
patronage, but the idols of the American

team are the descendants of the enslaved
my people too, so I wonder who to root for
in full.

*

We lost, Daddy says in disbelief and
my mother screeches in joy and I realize
we are all *we* in this moment, blazing
with our stupid American pride and as
we watch Puerto Rico prance across
the screen and Lebron hang his head
I wonder why I am so happy for Puerto Rico,
the underdog. I wonder why I am so distressed
for Lebron, I wonder about the space
between
a fork in a road.

Self-Portrait as Noah

byAmy Lee Heinlen

When the rain came, I had been dry for weeks.
When the land became an ocean lifting my boat,
I just wanted to relax with a nice bottle of red.
Just a taste to help ignore the mewling, moaning,
and stomping, that damn zebra who ate the oleander.
My thirst, an ocean to drown out the pounding,
the pleading after I secured the door.

beneath the lilacs by Sharon L. Green

Untitled by Robert Lozano

Kansas City Lights

by Jennifer Maritza McCauley

Touchdown or Something,
back to you crisping, lighted place
my swift escape, humble
glitz, jazz'd instrument
blowing quavers, shaking, from the cave
of your trumpet sounding like
all of my loving memories

of soaring ball and The Bird's winding
song, 18th & Vine. I watch the green of
your leafy fingers stretch into the ice-d
peace of Pittsburgh mind.

For years you've wound into my writings,
and here you are, open and waiting,
I find you as if I've known you long ago,
in my father's birth soil, I sing his
elegies and hard bops and shadows
but let me tell you something

this time the notes are mine.

When Jennifer Aniston was Married to Brad Pitt

by Amy Lee Heinlen

I don't know when exactly
or where I read the interview
or why but I remember her
idea of a satisfying evening
included going to bed early with
a big bottle of purified water

All these years since
I still think about that—
how we're able to become
accustomed to our surroundings
no matter how beautiful

Untitled by Cottonbro

We Are Like Jazz

by Jennifer Maritza McCauley

It don't mean a thing, if it ain't got a—trap. Snap. Then it's done.

"I'm yours. I'll see you," you say but I see you. See. I won't wait long.

You always tell me to find you without telling me where you'll go. Mostly you find me, deep in grey town, in a coffee spot alone and sometimes you come to see me but then you're gone quick.

There's no commitment to your rhythm. Tell me, honey, how you gonna ride that beat if you're fucking air? Billie Holiday suffered so much before she died and I sing her songs for you.

This music, our mirror stage, won't start nor end. I'll see you, sometimes I do, sometimes I don't but you keep playing your damn songs.

Louis said if you have to say what jazz is, you don't know what it is. Miles said, "Man, sometimes it takes you a long time to sound like yourself" and I don't know how we'll sound today or tomorrow, or how this jazz is going to keep spiking and striking and crying sin, but let me tell you,

no matter what, I got it going, got it going on.

Untitled by Rafael Romero

Editor Biographies

Madison Whatley is a South Florida poet and 2023 graduate of Florida International University's MFA program, where she was the managing editor at *Gulf Stream Magazine*. Her poetry has appeared in *Variant Literature*, *Cola Literary Review*, *Saw Palm: Florida Literature and Art*, and various other journals. Her manuscript "Hotline Bimbo" was selected as a Semifinalist for the 2023 Berkshire Prize for a First or Second Book of Poetry by Tupelo Press.

Yael Valencia Aldana is an award-winning poet and writer. She is the author of the poetry collection *Black Mestiza* and the chapbook *Alien(s)*. She is a Pushcart Prize winner, and her work has appeared in *Torch Literary Arts*, *Literary Mama*, and *Slag Glass City*, among others. She teaches creative writing in South Florida and is the managing editor of Purple Ink Press. She lives near the ocean with her son and too many pets. You can find her online at YaelAldana.com.

Contributor Biographies

Terri Watrous Berry is a Michigan septuagenarian whose work has appeared over the past thirty five years in anthologies, journals, magazines, and newspapers, and has been presented awards from venues as diverse as The Hemingway Days Festival and the Des Plaines/Park Ridge NOW Feminist Writer's Competition.

Arnaldo Batista is a queer, Latinx, Floridian poet who makes sense of the world through his writing. His work can be found in *Prairie Schooner*, *Slag Glass City,* and the *Gulf Coast Journal*. He has also been nominated for The Pushcart Prize in Nonfiction for 2024.

Hannah Birss is a writer and aspiring magpie based out of Ontario, Canada. She lives with her partner, children, and multiple animals. She can usually be found in a nest constructed of books, writing journals, and shiny trinkets. Follow her on Instagram at @hannahbirsswrites or at hannahbirsswrites.carrd.co for news on upcoming and current publications, with 26 and counting.

Kathy Bruce is a visual artist based in Argyll and Bute, Scotland. Her sculpture installations and collages trace the mythologies and histories of women, plants, and landscape, as well as how their interconnected relationships can be integrated visually to form a poetic contemporary understanding of Humans and Nature.

Moriah Brown is a poet, novelist, and full-time student at Syracuse University working towards a degree in creative writing. Her poetry has been published in the *Alchemy and Miracles Anthology, Creation Magazine, The Woolf, and The Passionfruit Review*, among others. She is from Fort Worth, Texas, and loves writing, birds, and her cat Nala.

Anjanette Delgado was born in Puerto Rico and writes about sexile, heartbreak and uprootedness. She is the Emmy award-winning author of two novels *The Heartbreak Pill* (Atria, 2008) and *The Clairvoyant of Calle Ocho* (Penguin Random House, 2014), and of the nonfiction hybrid, *El sexilio* (LaCriba, 2024). She has written poetry, fiction, and nonfiction for the *New York Times* (Modern Love; Opinion), *Vogue, NPR, HBO, Kenyon Review, Prairie Schooner, The Rumpus, Tupelo Quarterly, Pleiades Magazine,* and *the Boston Review*, among others. Anjanette is the editor of *Home in Florida: Latinx Writers and the Literature of Uprootedness* (University of Florida Press, 2021), the first anthology to gather Latinx voices in that state. It was chosen by "Poets & Writers" as one of three notable anthologies in 2021 and was a Gold Medal Winner for ensemble fiction at the Latino International Book Awards. She holds an MFA in Creative Writing from Florida International University and lives in Miami, Florida.

Denise Duhamel's most recent books of poetry are *Pink Lady* (Pitt Poetry Series, 2025), *Second Story* (2021), and *Scald* (2017). *Blowout* (2013) was a finalist for the National Book Critics Circle Award. She is a distinguished university professor in the MFA program at Florida International University in Miami and lives in Hollywood.

Alyssa Favreau is a Tiohtià:ke/Montreal-based editor for the McGill-Queen's University Press and the author of *Janelle Monáe's The Archandroid (33 1/3)*. Her work has appeared in *Hazlitt, the Los Angeles Times, In the Mood,* and the *Capilano Review,* among others.

Eleni Gemitzis, born in 1997, has a Master's degree in English and Philosophy/Ethics. After studying in Stuttgart, Coventry, and Rome, she is currently in teacher training. She loves every single bird in Virginia Woolf's novels, queer literature in general, and being in good company wherever she goes, including the digital space at@elenigemitzis.

Anyély Gómez-Dickerson is a Cuban-born poet/author with degrees from FIU in Miami and Temple University. Her poem "How to Kill a Mango Tree" was a finalist in Atlanta Review's 2023 Poetry Competition. Her work appears in *Latino Book Review, Acentos, the South Florida Poetry Journal,* and *West Trestle Review,* and her poetry collection We Are the Cultivated Sins was on exhibit at ARTE LATINO NOW 2024, where she's honored to share space with amazing authors. After a decades-long career empowering students through writing, her work probes issues plaguing marginalized communities, immigrant experiences, and the Afro-Caribbean diaspora while exploring her own black, European, and Taína ancestry.

Sharon L. Green is an artist, writer, and poet. Her life has become about art and poetry as her language. She has rediscovered her love for all things artistic and is self-taught, sketching, writing poetry, and painting her way through her days. She currently shares her residence between the forgotten coastline in Florida at her beach cottage and her home in a hamlet of Nashville, Tennessee called Leiper's Fork – renowned for their artsy eclectic village. "Given to me is beauty that surrounds, life beholding the verdant green. Bounty in treasures that I cannot hold, this life I lead." *Sharon L. Green.*

Marianna Faynshteyn (she/her) was born in Ukraine and moved to New York as a young child. While she had originally worked in journalism, she transitioned into digital advertising and now works in product   management. For the last nine years, she has lived in Amsterdam.

Venus Fultz is a non-binary writer (xe/xem) who enjoys prodding and pushing the boundaries of form and genre in writing. He received his MFA in Fiction at the University of Alaska, Fairbanks. His creative work can be found at *Marrow*

Magazine, *Wrongdoing Magazine, Resurrection Magazine, Queer As F*ck Anthology 3*, and more. He enjoys cooking and writing sappy love poems to the Moon.

Amy Lee Heinlen iis a poet and publisher living in Western Pennsylvania. Her first chapbook, All Else Falls to Shadow, was published by Dancing Girl Press. Her individual poems can be found in *Literary Mama, poets.org, Rogue Agent, Stirring: A Literary Collective, Glass: A Journal of Poetry, MER*, and elsewhere. Heinlen is co-founder and editor of Lefty Blondie Press, an independent publisher of handbound, hand-cut, and hand-numbered chapbooks and broadsides promoting self-identifying women and non-binary poets. Heinlen is the recipient of an Academy of American Poets University and College Prize and Best Thesis in Poetry prize from Chatham University.

Joe Hilliard. Writer. Luddite. Teller of Tales. He grew up as a teen in Los Angeles on a diet of Blue Demon, Doc Savage, Philip K. Dick, the Circle Jerks, Mildred Pierce, Judge Dredd, and 50s science fiction films, on the fringe of 80s Hollywood. He is a graduate of the University of Michigan, which only added Kawabata, Krazy Kat, and William S. Burroughs to the mix. He marks time as a paralegal in sunny California.

Salem B. Holden, like their gender, can be found everywhere and nowhere, probably hugging some tree in the woods, talking to spiders and praising them on their beautiful webs, or foraging for mushrooms. They've completed three chapbooks, How to They/them, Life in the Body, and Rebirth, and have been published in *Babyteeth, Many Nice Donkeys* and *Lions Online.* Their collages have been featured in SOS ART Cincinnati's Pride Celebration and won the R.M. Miller Fiction award twice for their YA novel.

Halsey Hyer is the author of the full-length collection *Divorce Garter* (Main Street Rag) and *[deadname]* (Anhinga Press), which won the Rick Campbell Chapbook

Prize, as well as the Pushcart Prize nominated micro-chapbook of micro-poems, *Everything Becomes Bananas* (Rinky Dink Press). Follow Halsey at halseyhyer.org or on Instagram at @enjoytheprocessoffuckingup.

Elizabeth Kandall, received her MFA in Poetry from Queens University of Charlotte where Ada Limón was her thesis advisor. She is a Poetry Editor at ROOM: *A Sketchbook for Analytic Action* and serves on the Board of Directors at Poets House. Her work as a psychologist and psychoanalyst is based in NY.

Frances Koziar has published prose and poetry in over 100 different literary magazines and outlets and has had over 20 professional-rate publications, including *Best Canadian Essays 2021* and *Daily Science Fiction*. She has also served as an author panelist, fiction contest judge, and microfiction editor. She is a young, (disabled) retiree and a social justice activist, and she lives in Kingston, Ontario, Canada. Her website is franceskoziar.wixsite.com/author.

Nona Lea authors essays on mythos, ecology, and literature, hosts poetry workshops, edits at *Vial of Bones Zine*, and is earning an MFA at Stonecoast. Lea has been published in over 13 literary magazines and volumes. *Melodia* is their debut poetry collection. Follow Lea at linktr.ee/nona_lea.

Melissa Ford Lucken is a professor of creative writing and composition at Lansing Community College, where she serves as the faculty editor of *The Washington Square Review*, the college's literary journal. She publishes commercial fiction, including erotic romance and erotic horror as Isabelle Drake.

Kristin Marie is a writer and writing instructor who resides in Florida. Her work has appeared in *Prairie Schooner, the South Florida Poetry Journal, Saw Palm: Florida Literature and Art,,* and elsewhere.

Sophie Mulgrew is an interdisciplinary writer and artist based out of NYC. She is interested in representations of nonfiction across different mediums. Her work has been published in *Thin Air Magazine, Papers Publishing, The Gallatin Review, Museé Magazine*, and more. Find her on Instagram at @thesophisticatedscrapbook.

Sharlyn Page is a life-long poet and philosopher residing in Florida, who has just begun to publish her works. Ten different publications have accepted her poetry in the last two years, and she has two books of poems in progress, and she has recently been nominated for the Pushcart Prize.

m. v. riasanovsky (they/them) is a nonbinary, queer poet and artist living in the foothills of the Appalachian Mountains (Central Virginia). They have self-published several zines and were a core part of the DIY poetry and performance community on their undergraduate campus (such as performing in The Vagina Monologues, organizing a campus zine fest, and editing a literary magazine). They are currently a grant writer at a local nonprofit and are passionate about mutual liberation and leftist movements.

Carolyn Schlam is a painter, sculptor, glass artist and published author. Carolyn's published books on art include *The Creative Path: A View from the Studio on the Making of Art and The Joy of Art: How to Look at, Appreciate, and Talk About Art*. Two additional books are forthcoming. Her artwork has appeared in many museums, art galleries, and publications, most notably in the Smithsonian Museum. Carolyn resides in southern California.

Jen Schneider is an educator who lives, writes, and works in small spaces throughout Pennsylvania. She served as the 2022 Montgomery County (PA) Poet Laureate. Her most recent collections, *14 (Plus) Reasons Why* (free lines press) and *Evening Walks* (ethel) are now available.

Liam Strong (they/them) is a queer, neurodivergent, and straight edge punk writer who has earned their BA in writing from the University of Wisconsin-Superior. They are the author of the chapbook *Everyone's Left the Hometown Show* (Bottlecap Press, 2023). You can find their poetry and essays in *Vagabond City* and *new words* {press}, among others. They are most likely gardening and listening to Bitter Truth somewhere in Northern Michigan. Find them on Instagram/Twitter at @ beanbie666.

Lauren Tivey is the author of four chapbooks, most recently *Moroccan Holiday* (winner of The Poetry Box Chapbook Prize 2019). Her full-length collection, *Traveler in the Sunset Clouds*, and her hybrid poetry/photography collaboration, *Fire Carousel*, were recently released by Main Street Rag Publishing Company. Her work appears in *Connotation Press, LETTERS, Dorothy Parker's Ashes*, and *Grimoire*. She teaches at Flagler College in St. Augustine, Florida.

Dylana Wagorn (it/they) is trying a lot of new things recently, both in life and in its writing practice right now. They write a lot of poetry and are attempting to make tabletop games.

Terin Weinberg earned her MFA from Florida International University (FIU) in Miami, Florida. She teaches in the English Departments at DeSales University and Northampton Community College in Pennsylvania. Her work has been previously published and anthologized by journals such as The Normal School, Flyway: Journal for Writing & Environment, Split Rock Review, and more. When she isn't teaching and writing, Terin is farming with her husband.

Kaitlyn Whatley is a Queer artist born and raised in South Florida. She is pursuing a minor in fine arts and a bachelor's in political science at Louisiana State University. She resides in Baton Rouge, LA, where she enjoys LSU Tigers football. Her work has been featured in publications such as *805 Lit + Art* and *GulfStream*.

Madison Whatley is a South Florida poet and 2023 graduate of Florida International University's MFA program, where she was the managing editor at Gulf Stream Magazine. Her poetry has appeared in *Variant Literature, Cola Literary Review, Saw Palm: Florida Literature and Art*, and various other journals. Her manuscript "Hotline Bimbo" was selected as a Semifinalist for the 2023 Berkshire Prize for a First or Second Book of Poetry by Tupelo Press.